GLUTEN-FREE
food for kids

GLUTEN-FREE
food for kids

**More than 100 quick & easy
recipes for children**

Louise Blair

hamlyn

An Hachette UK Company
www.hachette.co.uk

First published in Great Britain in 2015 by
Hamlyn, a division of Octopus Publishing Group Ltd
Carmelite House
50 Victoria Embankment
London EC4Y 0DZ
www.octopusbooks.co.uk
www.octopusbooksusa.com

Distributed in the US by
Hachette Book Group
1290 Avenue of the Americas
4th and 5th Floors
New York, NY 10020

Distributed in Canada by
Canadian Manda Group
664 Annette St.
Toronto, Ontario, Canada M6S 2C8

Louise Blair asserts the moral right to be identified as the author of this work

ISBN 978 0 60063 222 1

Printed and bound in China

10 9 8 7 6 5 4 3 2 1

Standard level kitchen spoon and cup measurements are used in all recipes.

Ovens should be preheated to the specified temperature; if using a convection oven,
follow the manufacturer's instructions for adjusting the time and temperature.

Fresh herbs should be used unless otherwise stated.

Large eggs should be used unless otherwise stated.

The U.S. Food and Drug Administration advises that eggs should not be consumed
raw. This book contains some dishes made with raw or lightly cooked eggs. It is
prudent for vulnerable people, such as pregnant and nursing mothers, people
with weakened immune systems, the elderly, babies, and young children to avoid
uncooked or lightly cooked dishes made with eggs. Once prepared, these dishes
should be kept refrigerated and used promptly.

This book includes dishes made with nuts and nut derivatives. It is advisable
for those with known allergic reactions to nuts and nut derivatives and those
who may be potentially vulnerable to these allergies to avoid dishes made
with nuts and nut oils. It is also prudent to check the labels of prepared
ingredients for the possible inclusion of nut derivatives.

This book is meant to be used as a general reference and recipe guide for gluten-free food.
However, you are urged to consult a health-care professional to check whether a gluten-free diet
is suitable for you or your children before embarking on it. While all reasonable care has been taken
during the preparation of this edition, the information it contains is not intended to take the place
of advice or treatment by a health-care professional. Neither the publishers, editors, nor the
author can accept responsibility for any consequences arising from the use of the information
in this book.

contents

introduction

Being diagnosed with a lifelong condition such as celiac disease can be extremely daunting to an adult, but for a child it can be even more stressful and upsetting. This book aims to show you and your child that such a diagnosis doesn't have be the end of the world, and your child shouldn't feel different or be excluded from the things that others take for granted.

If you have a child who has been diagnosed with celiac disease, remember that there is a lot of assistance out there to help. Once your child has received the correct support and education and follows a gluten-free diet, symptoms will improve and he or she can live a normal life.

What is gluten?

Gluten is a protein that is found in a number of grains, including wheat, barley, and rye. Due to cross-contamination during the processing of some oats, they, too, can contain gluten. Gluten gives dough its "stretch," helping give stability and shape and giving the end product its desirable "chewiness." Given that grains containing gluten are the main ingredient in many popular and staple food items, such as breads, cookies, and cakes, being told that these are now a "no-go" area may seem overwhelming or impossible, and finding suitable alternatives may be challenging. What we aim to show you in this book is that there is life beyond gluten—and a delicious one, too.

What is celiac disease?

Contrary to common misconceptions, celiac disease is not a food allergy or a food intolerance; it is an autoimmune disease whereby the body makes antibodies against the protein "gluten." Antibodies that are usually responsible for attacking bacteria and viruses detect the gluten and attack it, thus causing inflammation of the lining of the small intestine.

Causes and symptoms

The lining of the small intestine is covered with millions of tiny fingerlike projections called villi. When antibodies attack the gluten in foods, they cause inflammation, which in turn flattens the villi, meaning that nutrients from food cannot be so readily absorbed. This can result in deficiencies, including anemia.

Other symptoms range from mild to severe and can include diarrhea, bloating, abdominal pain, excess gas, and tiredness or weakness. Often the symptoms of celiac disease are confused with irritable bowel syndrome (IBS) or a wheat intolerance, because the symptoms can be similar. Symptoms can vary from person to person. In infants, celiac disease may be indicated if the child is not thriving; in children, it can cause a lack of appetite, altered bowel habits, and anamia; and within the adult population

pita chips, page 47

symptoms include anemia, diarrhea, chronic tiredness and lethargy, weight loss, and other abdominal abnormalities. Other body systems can also be affected, resulting in headaches, hair loss, tooth enamel erosion, and joint pain. Long-term problems caused by untreated or undiagnosed celiac disease can lead to the following:

- Infertility in women, including recurrent miscarriage
- Poor growth of babies during pregnancy
- Osteoporosis—thinning of bones
- An increased risk of bowel cancer, intestinal lymphoma, and cancer of the esophagus.

A gluten-free diet reduces these complications as well as other associated conditions, such as canker sores and dermatitis herpetiformis. Sticking to a gluten-free diet will also reduce the risk of any cancers associated with celiac disease and bring these occurances in line with statistics for the normal population.

Who has celiac disease?

About 1 in 133 people living in the United States are affected by celiac disease, which is more than two million people in the population. Anyone, at any age, can develop celiac disease. People of European descent, especially from northern European countries, have a greater risk of developing the disease; however, recent research shows it also affects people of Hispanic, African, and Asian descent. Celiac disease is hereditary. If you have a close family member, such as a parent, child, or sibling, who has celiac disease, you have a 1 in 10 chance of having or developing celiac disease. If your child has another autoimmune disease—for example, some thyroid diseases, rheumatoid arthritis, or type 1 diabetes—he or she is also more at risk of having or developing celiac disease.

Diagnosis and treatment

If you suspect your child has celiac disease, don't remove gluten from his or her diet immediately. First of all, consult your physician, who will carry out a simple blood test to detect if the antibody against gluten is present. If this blood test is positive, your child may be referred for a biopsy of the lining of the small intestine to determine if the tell-tale signs of celiac disease are present. If you remove gluten from your child's diet before he or she is tested, the test may produce a negative result.

If your child tests positive, the next step is to completely cut out gluten from his or her diet for life. Symptoms will usually disappear within a couple of weeks and the small intestine will begin to repair itself. Symptoms will return, however, even if only a tiny amount of gluten is consumed. Your physician should refer you to a dietitian, who can give you advice on how to deal with celiac disease and what your child should and should not eat. Look for support organizations on the Internet. Celiac.com (www.celiac.com) provides not only advice, but also lists of safe gluten-free foods and unsafe ingredients. Celiiac Disease Foundation (www.celiac.org) has a list of organizations around the world that can help if you plan to travel out of the country.

Manufacturers occasionally change ingredients or suppliers and therefore a product that was previously gluten-free may change to contain gluten, so always check the ingredients on the labels. Look for gluten-free labeling.

Children and celiac disease

Children and their siblings of all ages need to recognize their diagnosis, understanding why their bodies act in a different way when exposed to gluten and how this relates to how well they feel. Children have an amazing ability to adapt and with the right help and support this lifestyle change should be easily attained.

A meeting with school teachers, catering staff, and the school nurse is essential. Schools are required to make arrangements to support children so meeting all involved is a good way to ensure that this is done and that appropriate support is in place. Celiac Disease Foundation provides guidance on how to file a 504 Plan to ensure your child qualifies for special dietary requirements in the National School Lunch Program. The organization also provides advice on what to pack in a gluten-free lunch box, lists of gluten-free candies by holiday, such as Halloween and Easter, and information on gluten-free sleepaway camps.

The most important thing to remember is that your child is not alone—there are a lot of other kids in the same situation and many people to help and guide them.

Introducing a gluten-free diet

Gluten is present in all wheat, barley, and rye products, and sometimes in oats through cross-contamination, so careful thought needs to be given to shopping for, preparing, and cooking a gluten-free diet for your child.

USDA regulations stipulate that manufacturers can label products as gluten-free only when there is less than 20 parts per million of gluten per product (considered by health experts as a safe level). However, not all gluten-free products are labeled as such, so check the ingredients list to identify if any products containing gluten are used.

Some foods that contain gluten are obvious—for example, breads, cakes, pastries, cookies, and pasta. Others, such as processed foods, including some candies, chocolate, soups, potato chips, and sausages, may also contain gluten, so a good study of food labels is essential.

Don't panic. Take a look at all the foods that are naturally gluten-free (see right) and you will see that these can be used to make delicious meals. A quick read through the recipes in this book will also reveal that gluten-free cooking can still be exciting, simple, easy, and delicious.

banana tarte tartin, page 122

Naturally gluten-free foods

- Fruits and vegetables, including potatoes
- Unprocessed meat, poultry, and fish (including shellfish)
- Unprocessed cheeses, butter, milk, and plain milk products, including cream
- Eggs
- Tofu
- Cooking oils
- Sugar, baking soda, cream of tartar, and yeast
- Plain nuts, seeds, and legumes (dried beans, lentils, and chickpeas)
- Rice and associated rice products, such as rice noodles and rice flour
- Gluten-free grains and their associated products, such as buckwheat noodles, grits, cornstarch, and cornmeal*
- Plain yogurt
- Vinegars
- Fats
- Coffee and tea
- Herbs and spices

*NB: Some naturally gluten-free grains are milled with wheat, barley, and rye, and therefore may be cross-contaminated with grains that do contain gluten; always read the package label.

Foods that contain gluten

- Wheat, barley, and rye and their products, such as pasta, wheat noodles, bulgur wheat, and couscous
- Breads, cakes, cookies, breakfast cereals, and snacks/confectionery containing wheat, barley, and rye flour
- Baking powder
- Foods covered in batter, bread crumbs, or dusted with flour
- Some soft drinks and malted milk drinks
- Some mustard products may contain wheat as a thickener
- Chinese soy sauce, which is traditionally made from fermented wheat
- Stuffing mixes
- Some store-bought prepared seasonings, sauces, soups, gravy granules, and bouillon cubes
- Some sausages contain wheat husk

Gluten-free store-bought alternatives

As well as the basic foodstuffs that are gluten-free, you can also buy prepared food items that use gluten-free ingredients as a substitute for those containing gluten. As there is an increasingly awareness of the needs for a gluten-free diet, food manufacturers have been creating a growing range of gluten-free products, such as breads, cookies, pasta, and even meatball and hotdogs. Many of these products have come a long way from the bland, poor-quality gluten-free foods of years gone by and are often available even at smaller stores or online.

Gluten-free products are not always the same as traditional goods, however, because it is gluten that gives bread its elasticity and cakes their spring. If you try one product and your child doesn't like it, don't worry— try another brand or get baking yourself. You will be surprised when you sample some of the carefully selected recipes in this book that gluten-free ingredients can replicate relatively closely many of the foods that contain gluten.

banana & peanut brownies, page 96

Pantry essentials

As mentioned before, there are many naturally gluten-free products, such as unprocessed meat and fish, dairy foods, fresh fruit and vegetables, rice, and legumes. However, you will need to prepare other common foods that are not normally gluten-free—such as white sauce, gravy, cakes, breads, and pasta and noodle dishes—using gluten-free ingredients. If you look for and stock up on some of the following items, you will be able to make all the recipes in this book whenever you want.

Flours

As well as certain flour mixes, there are other gluten-free flours that can be used for baking and cooking, such as rice, chickpea (besan), potato, soy, corn, buckwheat, and millet. If these flours are not available in your local supermarket, they can usually be found in health-food stores or ordered online. You don't need to buy them all, for general all-purpose use, rice flour is a great all-rounder and cornstarch is good for sauces and thickening stews, although it is worth experimenting with other flours as well. This book primarily uses rice flour and cornstarch.

Xanthan gum

A powder that greatly aids gluten-free baking, xanthan gum, to some extent, replaces the elastic qualities that gluten-free flours lack. Adding a little to gluten-free flours makes bread less crumbly and gluten-free pastry easier to roll and handle. It's available in speciality health-food stores and in some supermarkets. Xanthan gum are in these recipes only where it is really needed—use a variety or mixture of other flours can produce the best results. It is often used in bread recipes, biscuits, and scones, as well as cakes and cookies.

Gluten-free baking powder

Standard, store-bought baking powder contains gluten, but gluten-free baking powder is now available in the baking sections of most larger supermarkets. If you prefer, you can make your own gluten-free baking powder with baking soda and cream of tartar which are both naturally gluten-free. Simply mix two parts baking soda with one part cream of tartar and use the mixture spoon for spoon in baking, as you would with a standard, store-bought baking powder.

Pasta and noodles

Gluten-free pastas are becoming more common, and are marketed as such. Rice noodles are gluten-free, as are the varieties of soba noodles that are made entirely from buckwheat.

Grains

Quinoa is a wonderful addition to the diet, providing an excellent source of protein as well as being gluten-free. It is a great substitute for couscous or bulgur wheat in salads and side dishes. Grits are good for baking and for use as an alternative coating to bread crumbs. As a form of carbohydrate, it can also be used in place of pasta.

Legumes

Lentils, beans, and chickpeas can be used in stews and casseroles but are also great in salads or as side dishes.

Cheese and dairy

Unprocessed cheeses are gluten-free and wonderful to have on hand in the refrigerator; don't overuse, though, because they are high in fat. Milk and plain, unflavored yogurts are gluten-free, and it is worth looking at the labels of other dairy products to find gluten-free options.

As with all types of cooking, gluten-free cooking can be a case of trial and error, because gluten-free products have different baking qualities and properties. Don't give up if you find that you don't instantly get good results—you will achieve acceptable results eventually. As well as providing a satisfying gluten-free diet for your child, rest assured that the rest of the family will also be more than happy with the recipes in this book.

Cross-contamination

So you have cut out gluten from your child's diet, found your way around the gluten-free products available, and have the gluten-free foods list on hand (*see* page 8), so all should be plain sailing from here. You, your child, and your family must be aware, however, that cross-contamination is easy: by spreading butter that has been contaminated with "normal" bread crumbs on gluten-free toast; by using

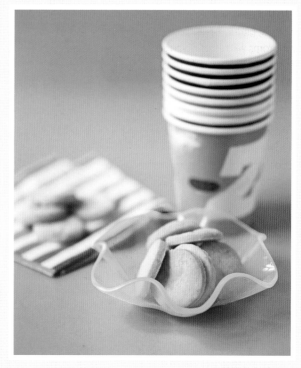

cheesy bites, page 126

the same toaster for gluten-free and "normal" bread; or by stirring a gluten-free dish with a spoon that has been stirring gravy made with wheat flour. Even small amounts of gluten can cause the symptoms of celiac disease to return. Make the following simple but important tips a part of your cooking routine in order to prevent cross-contamination:

• Store gluten-free flours separately
• Use separate utensils to prepare gluten-free food
• Keep a "gluten-free" sifter or strainer, rolling pin, pastry brush, and cutting board
• Wash everything well and always clean surfaces before cooking and eating.

It is often easier to cook one gluten-free dish for the whole family; it takes less time and involves less risk of cross-contamination.

Day-to-day life

Avoiding gluten is for life. If your child eats gluten again, symptoms will return. Even small amounts of gluten can resensitize the digestive tract. To avoid symptoms returning and additional complications, your child must be strict about avoiding all foods containing gluten (*see* page 8).

Start the way you mean to go on. Involve your child in choosing suitable foodstuffs and ingredients and how to prepare them without risking cross-contamination. Mark foods with stickers stating whether they are gluten-free or not and make sure they understand, if they are old enough, about cross-contamination (see left). If involved from the beginning, it will quickly become routine and your child will be more aware when away from you.

Holding children's parties

Keep the menu simple and serve the same food for all the children. There is a great selection of party foods in this cookbook, including cakes, cheesy bites, and cookies. If you don't have time to prepare it all yourself, however, you can supplement it with gluten-free store-bought foods, such as vegetables to make crudités to serve with gluten-free dips, fresh fruit, and hotdogs. There are several cake recipes in this book, such as the Chocolate Sponge with Buttercream on page 134, which can be easily adapted to your child's requests.

Carbonated beverages, fruit juices, and many clear soft drinks do not contain gluten, but check any cloudy beverages because these may contain barley.

Away from home
Parties and play dates

When your child is going on a play date or to a party, you will need to liaise with the other parents or organizer. While it is important to give your child the independence to manage his or her own diet, when away from home your child may not be too sure about all the food offered. For peace of mind, you may find it easier to pack up some food for your child. Ask what types of party food are being prepared so you can substitute similar gluten-free versions. Perhaps you could bring along gluten-free alternatives for everyone to try so your child feels included.

Eating out

Check the menu of restaurants where you plan to eat and make sure that staff are aware of your child's condition prior to your visit. Hidden gluten can be in sauces, coatings (for example, bread crumbs), gravy, and bouillon cubes. Many chefs are happy to cook something not on the menu for your child with your advice.

Cooking at school

With careful planning, there is no reason why your child cannot take part in cooking at school. Get a step ahead of the game and liaise with the class teacher to be sure that you child is able to use utensils that haven't come into contact with gluten. You could also provide a gluten-free recipe for the whole class to make, which will help to eliminate the risk of cross-contamination.

Making mistakes

If your child eats gluten by mistake, some symptoms will usually start to appear a few hours after eating, and the effects can last from a few hours to several days, depending on your child's sensitivity to what he or she has eaten. You may want to treat the symptoms or prefer to wait until they naturally get better. If your child is experiencing diarrhea or is vomiting, it is important to keep him or her well hydrated by making sure they drink plenty of water. Some people also find that taking medication to treat constipation, diarrhea, or headaches can ease symptoms, so speak to your pharmacist or physician. The most important thing is to get your child back on to a gluten-free diet as soon as possible to try to prevent additional symptoms. If your child's symptoms are severe or do not improve, discuss them with your physician.

breakfast

yogurt & berry smoothie

Serves 4

Preparation time 5 minutes

1¼ cups plain yogurt

4 cups fresh or 1 (1 lb) package frozen
  mixed berries, such as raspberries,
  hulled strawberries, and blackberries,
  defrosted if frozen, plus extra
  to decorate

¼ cup millet flakes

3 tablespoons honey

1¼ cups cranberry juice

Millet flakes are an excellent source of magnesium, while the berries provide plenty of vitamin C for healthy kids.

1 Place all the ingredients in a food processor or a blender and process until smooth.

2 Pour into 4 glasses, decorate with a few extra whole berries, and serve immediately.

tropical fruit smoothie

Serves 4

Preparation time 10 minutes

1 mango, peeled, pitted, and chopped

2 kiwifruits, peeled and chopped

1 banana, cut into chunks

1 (15 oz) can pineapple chunks or pieces in natural juice

2 cups orange or apple juice

handful of ice cubes

This is like sunshine in a glass and provides an easy breakfast on the go, or midmorning energy boost.

1 Place all the ingredients in a food processor or blender and process until smooth.

2 Pour into 4 glasses and serve immediately.

bircher muesli

Serves 4

**Preparation time 5 minutes,
plus overnight soaking**

4 cups buckwheat flakes

1¼ cups milk

½ cup apple juice

1 apple, peeled and grated

2 tablespoons honey

⅔ cup dried fruit, such as mango,
apricots, or golden raisins

1 cup hazelnuts, toasted and
coarsely chopped

poached or canned fruit, such as
peaches or berries, to serve

1 Mix together the buckwheat flakes, milk, apple juice, and grated apple in a bowl. Cover and let soak overnight.

2 To serve, stir the honey, dried fruit, and nuts into the muesli mixture. Spoon into bowls, then top with the poached or canned fruit and serve.

Hints and tips

You can try this recipe with any of your favorite dried fruit and nuts, or sprinkle with flaked dried coconut for a tropical flavor.

buckwheat porridge

Serves 4

Preparation time 5 minutes

Cooking time 5 minutes

4 cups buckwheat flakes

1 ripe banana, chopped

½ teaspoon ground cinnamon

⅔ cup golden raisins

¾ cup milk

1 cup water

honey, to serve

2 cups mixed berries, to serve

To vary the porridge, try replacing the banana with a chopped pear and serve with chopped toasted walnuts and honey.

1 Put all the ingredients into a saucepan over low heat and bring to a simmer, then cook gently for 3–4 minutes, until the flakes are tender.

2 Blend briefly with an immersion blender, then serve drizzled with a little honey.

breakfast cereal bars

Makes 16

Preparation time 10 minutes

Cooking time 35 minutes

1 stick butter, softened, plus extra for greasing

2 tablespoons packed light brown sugar

2 tablespoons light corn syrup

2¾ cups millet flakes

¼ cup quinoa

⅓ cup dried cherries or cranberries

½ cup golden raisins

3 tablespoons sunflower seeds

3 tablespoons sesame seeds

2½ tablespooons flaxseed

½ cup flaked unsweetened dried coconut

2 eggs, lightly beaten

1 Grease an 11 x 8 inch shallow baking pan.

2 Beat together the butter, sugar, and syrup in a large bowl until creamy. Add all the remaining ingredients and beat well until combined.

3 Spoon the batter into the prepared pan and level the surface with the back of the spoon. Place in a preheated oven, at 350°F, for 35 minutes, until deep golden. Let cool in the pan.

4 Turn out onto a wooden board and carefully cut into 16 bars using a serrated knife. Store in an airtight container for up to 5 days.

chewy tropical squares

Makes 9

Preparation time 10 minutes

Cooking time 20 minutes

butter, for greasing

⅔ cup chopped dates

⅓ cup chopped dried mango

⅔ cup chopped dried apricots

½ cup orange juice

½ cup almonds, skin on

1¾ cups ground almonds (almond meal)

⅔ cup mixed sunflower and
  pumpkin seeds

2 tablespoons flaked unsweetened
  dried coconut

2 tablespoons maple syrup

1 Lightly grease an 8 inch square baking pan.

2 Place the fruits and orange juice in a bowl. Soak for 5 minutes.

3 Transfer the mixture to a food processor or blender, add the whole almonds, and blend briefly so the mixture retains some texture. Stir in all the remaining ingredients, except the syrup.

4 Press the batter into the prepared pan and place in a preheated oven, at 350°F, for 20 minutes, until golden.

5 Brush with the maple syrup, then mark into 9 squares and let cool in the pan before turning out and breaking into squares.

6 Store in an airtight container for 2–3 days.

fruit-topped pancakes

Makes 8

Preparation time 10 minutes

Cooking time 10–15 minutes

3 extra-large eggs, separated

¾ cup brown rice flour

1 teaspoon gluten-free baking powder

1 tablespoon sugar

⅔ cup milk

butter, for frying

Topping

3 cups hulled and halved strawberries

1 tablespoon sugar

You can use any fruit, such as blackberries, plums, cherries, or fresh apricots, to top the pancakes. If you prefer traditional pancakes for breakfast, serve these with crispy fried bacon slices, drizzled with maple syrup.

1 Whisk together the egg yolks, flour, baking powder, sugar, and milk in a large bowl. Whisk the egg whites until stiff in a separate clean bowl, then fold into the flour mixture.

2 Stir together the strawberries and sugar and set aside while cooking the pancakes.

3 Heat a little butter in a skillet, spoon in tablespoons of the pancake batter, and cook for 1–2 minutes on each side, until bubbles appear and golden and puffed up. Remove from the pan and keep warm while you cook the remaining pancakes.

4 Serve the pancakes topped with the strawberries.

Hints and tips
It is important to use the batter immediately, because it will become too runny if left standing.

french toast with cinnamon apples

Serves 4

Preparation time 5 minutes

Cooking time 5 minutes

2 eggs

1 tablespoon sugar

2 tablespoons milk

few drops of vanilla extract

4 thick slices of gluten-free bread

2 tablespoons butter

Cinnamon apples

pat of butter, for frying

2 crisp sweet apples, peeled, cored, and finely sliced

1 tablespoon sugar

squeeze of lemon juice

½ tablespoon ground cinnamon

This is also delicious served as a dessert with dollops of vanilla ice cream, cream, or crème fraîche.

1 Beat together the eggs, sugar, milk, and vanilla extract in a shallow bowl. Dip the slices of bread into the egg mixture, making sure they are fully coated in the mixture.

2 Heat the butter in a large nonstick skillet, add the egg-soaked bread, and cook for 1–2 minutes on each side, until golden. Remove from the pan and keep warm.

3 Meanwhile, put all the cinnamon apple ingredients into a saucepan and cook gently for 4–5 minutes, until the apples are just tender.

4 Serve the french toast topped with the cinnamon apples.

french toast with chives

Serves 4

Preparation time 5 minutes

Cooking time 5 minutes

2 eggs, beaten

2 tablespoons milk

2 tablespoons grated Parmesan cheese

2 tablespoons snipped chives

4 thick slices of gluten-free bread

2 tablespoons butter

salt and black pepper

Try making this with the Basic White Loaf (*see* page 110)—it works well in this recipe. This French toast is delicious served topped with a poached egg, some crispy fried bacon, or a cooked gluten-free sausage.

1 Beat together the eggs, milk, Parmesan, and chives in a shallow bowl and season well. Dip the slices of bread into the egg mixture, making sure they are fully coated in the mixture.

2 Heat the butter in a large nonstick skillet, add the egg-soaked bread, and cook for 1–2 minutes on each side, until golden.

banana & date bread

Makes 1 loaf

Preparation time 10 minutes

Cooking time 1 hour

1 stick butter, softened, plus extra
  for greasing

¾ cup chopped dates

½ teaspoon baking soda

½ cup boiling water

2 teaspoons gluten-free baking powder

¾ cup rice flour

⅓ cup cornstarch

⅓ cup sugar

2 eggs, beaten

4 small ripe bananas, mashed

1 Grease and line a 9 x 5 x 3 inch loaf pan.

2 Put the dates and baking soda into a small bowl and pour the measured water over them. Set aside.

3 Beat together all the remaining ingredients in a large bowl. Pour the date mixture into the cake batter and stir well, then pour into the prepared pan.

4 Place in a preheated oven, at 325°F, for about 1 hour, until golden, risen, and a toothpick inserted into the center comes out clean. Cool on a wire rack (also delicious served warm).

Hints and tips

Try adding chocolate chips and a tablespoon of cocoa to the cake batter for a special treat, or experiment with raisins and other dried fruit, if you prefer.

waffles & fresh fruit

Serves 4

Preparation time 5 minutes, plus resting

Cooking time 10 minutes

¾ cup brown rice flour

1⅓ cups chickpea (besan) flour

2 teaspoons gluten-free baking powder

2 tablespoons sugar

1½ teaspoons xanthan gum

3 extra-large eggs, beaten

⅔ cup heavy cream

1½ cups milk

few drops of vanilla extract

1¼ sticks butter, melted and cooled

fresh strawberries or blueberries, to serve

If you don't have a waffle iron, you can make these as pancakes instead.

1 Mix together the flours, baking powder, sugar, and xantham gum in a large bowl. Whisk together all the remaining ingredients in a separate bowl, then pour the wet ingredients into the dry ingredients and beat to form a smooth batter. Cover with plastic wrap and let rest in the refrigerator for at least 1 hour or overnight.

2 Heat a waffle iron until hot, then pour in a small ladle of the batter, making sure you don't overfill the iron. Cook according to the manufacturer's directions until golden. Serve immediately, topped with fresh strawberries or blueberries.

3 Repeat with the remaining batter until all the batter is used.

mini tomato & feta omelets

Makes 12

Preparation time 10 minutes

Cooking time 10 minutes

melted butter, for greasing

4 eggs, beaten

2 tablespoons chopped chives

3 sun-dried tomatoes, finely sliced

½ cup crumbled feta cheese

salt and black pepper

1 Lightly brush a 12-cup mini muffin pan with melted butter.

2 Mix together all the remaining ingredients in a large bowl until just combined.

3 Pour the batter into the prepared pan and place in a preheated oven, at 425°F, for about 10 minutes, until golden and puffed up. Serve warm.

granola & blueberry compote yogurt

Serves 4

Preparation time 10 minutes, plus cooling

Cooking time 20 minutes

2 cups blueberries

¼ cup apple juice

1⅔ cups plain or Greek yogurt

Granola

¼ cup maple syrup, plus extra to serve

2 tablespoons Demerara or other raw sugar

2 tablespoons vegetable oil

2 cups mixed nuts, such as pecans, hazelnuts, and almonds, coarsely chopped

2 tablespoons sunflower seeds

4 cups buckwheat flakes

1 cup millet flakes

1 cup raisins or 1 cup other chopped dried fruit

1 Make the granola. Mix together the syrup, sugar, and oil in a large bowl, then add the nuts, seeds, and flakes and toss until well coated. Spread out on a large baking sheet and place in a preheated oven, at 350°F, for 10 minutes. Stir through the dried fruit and bake for an additional 10 minutes.

2 Meanwhile, put the blueberries and apple juice into a small saucepan and cook for a few minutes until the juices begin to run. Let cool.

3 Remove the granola from the oven and let cool. (It can be stored in an airtight container for up to 1 week.)

4 To serve, spoon a little of the yogurt into 4 tall glasses, then layer with the compote and tablespoons of granola. Finish with a layer of granola.

big breakfast muffins

Makes 12

Preparation time 10 minutes

Cooking time 20–25 minutes

4 bacon slices

1 gluten-free sausage

2 teaspoons olive oil, for frying

1½ cups chopped white mushrooms

1½ cups brown rice flour

1 teaspoon baking soda

2 teaspoons gluten-free baking powder

6 tablespoons butter, melted

2 eggs, beaten

⅔ cup buttermilk

salt and black pepper

1 Line a 12-cup muffin pan with paper muffin cups.

2 Cook the bacon and sausage under a preheated broiler on in a skillet until cooked through and the bacon is crisp. Let cool slightly, then crumble the bacon and thinly slice the sausage.

3 Meanwhile, heat a little oil in a skillet, add the mushrooms, and cook for about 5 minutes, until softened.

4 Sift the flour, baking soda, and baking powder into a large bowl, then add the bacon, sausage, and mushrooms and stir together. Whisk together the butter, eggs, and buttermilk in a separate bowl and season well, then pour into the dry ingredients and stir until just combined (leave the batter a little lumpy, because this will produce a better end result).

5 Spoon the batter into the muffin cups and place in a preheated oven, at 350°F, for 15–18 minutes, until golden and just firm to the touch. Serve warm.

lemon, orange & passion fruit curd

Makes 5 (8 oz) jars

Preparation time 10 minutes

Cooking time 10–15 minutes

8 passion fruit

grated zest of 3 lemons and juice of 5 lemons

grated zest and juice of 2 large oranges

1½ cups superfine sugar

1 stick butter, cubed

5 eggs, plus 2 egg yolks

1 Halve the passion fruit and push half of the flesh through a strainer into a bowl, discarding the seeds. Whisk together the passion fruit juice, the remaining passion fruit flesh, and the lemon and orange zest and juice in a medium heatproof bowl.

2 Add the sugar and butter to the bowl, then set over a saucepan of gently simmering water, stirring until melted. Stir in the eggs and continue to whisk for 10–15 minutes or until the mixture has thickened to the consistency of custard.

3 Pour the mixture into about 5 sterilized jars, seal tightly, and store in the refrigerator for up to 2 weeks.

Hints and tips

This is delicious served spread on gluten-free Soda Bread (*see* page 116), or swirled into plain yogurt for a zesty dessert.

snacks,
lunch boxes
& picnics

chicken & ham soup

Serves 8

Preparation time 20 minutes

Cooking time 1 hour 20 minutes

3 tablespoons olive oil

4 large skinless chicken thighs

3 onions, chopped

2 celery sticks, sliced

1 (12 oz) piece of lean cured ham, cut into ½ inch chunks

2 bay leaves

2½ cups gluten-free chicken broth

2½ cups water

3 Yukon gold or red-skinned potatoes, peeled and cut into small cubes

1 cup frozen corn kernels

Dumplings

1 cup fine cornmeal

⅔ cup gluten-free flour

2 teaspoons gluten-free baking powder

1 tablespoon chopped thyme

3 tablespoons cold butter

1 cup water

salt and black pepper

1 Heat the oil in a large, heavy saucepan, add the chicken, onions, and celery, and sauté gently for 10 minutes, stirring, until golden.

2 Add the ham, bay leaves, broth, and measured water and bring to a boil. Reduce the heat, cover, and simmer gently for 40 minutes, until the chicken and ham are tender.

3 Lift out the chicken with a slotted spoon and, when cool enough to handle, shred the flesh from the bones. Return the flesh to the pan with the potatoes and corn kernels. Simmer, covered, for 20 minutes, until the potatoes are tender.

4 Make the dumplings. Mix together the cornmeal, flour, baking powder, thyme, and salt and black pepper in a bowl until evenly combined. Grate the butter into the mixture and add the measured water. Mix to a thick paste, adding a little more water, if necessary.

5 Use 2 tablespoons to coarsely pat the paste into 8 disks and spoon into the soup. Cover and simmer gently for about 10 minutes, until the dumplings are light and puffy.

tomato & red pepper soup with crunchy croutons

Serves 4–6

Preparation time 10 minutes

Cooking time 20 minutes

2 tablespoons olive oil

1 onion, chopped

1 garlic clove, crushed

1 large carrot, peeled and chopped

2 red bell peppers, cored, seeded, and cut into chunks

handful of basil, stems chopped and leaves torn

8 ripe tomatoes (about 2 lb), coarsely chopped

4 cups gluten-free chicken or vegetable broth

½ cup heavy cream

salt and black pepper

Croutons

2 thick slices of gluten-free bread, cubed

2 tablespoons grated Parmesan cheese

2 tablespoons olive oil

1 Heat the oil in a large saucepan, add the onion, garlic, carrot, red bell peppers, and basil stems, and sauté for 3–4 minutes, until beginning to soften. Add the tomatoes and broth and bring to a boil, then reduce the heat and simmer for 15 minutes, until the vegetables are tender.

2 Meanwhile, toss the bread cubes in the Parmesan and oil, then add to a skillet and cook over medium heat until golden.

3 Transfer the vegetable mixture to a food processor or blender and process until smooth. Return to the pan, stir in the cream, and season to taste. Reheat gently if necessary.

4 Ladle the soup into bowls, top with the torn basil, and serve with the croutons.

Hints and tips

If you prefer a heartier soup, add a can of beans, such as cannellini (white kidney) beans once the soup is cooked and serve topped with fried chorizo pieces.

zingy shrimp wraps

Makes 12

Preparation time 15 minutes

12 rice wrappers

5 oz cooked peeled shrimp, shredded

1 carrot, peeled and cut into
fine matchsticks

¼ cucumber, cut into fine matchsticks

1 small bunch of fresh cilantro, chopped

8 mint leaves, chopped

½ mango, peeled and cut into small strips

1 teaspoon sesame oil

1 teaspoon lime juice

handful of peanuts, coarsely chopped
(optional)

½ red chile, seeded and finely chopped
(optional)

These wraps are a great way to introduce kids to some fresh, Asian-inspired flavors.

1 Prepare the rice wrappers according to the package directions.

2 Toss together all the remaining ingredients in a bowl. Divide the mixture evenly among the wrappers and roll up, making sure the ends are tucked in. Serve immediately.

cheese & onion crepes

Makes 4

Preparation time 15 minutes

Cooking time 10 minutes

½ cup chickpea (besan) flour

⅓ cup rice flour

½ teaspoon xanthan gum

3 tablespoons olive oil

1 cup water

handful of fresh cilantro, chopped

½ chile, seeded and finely chopped (optional)

1 garlic clove, finely sliced

a little oil, for frying

1 cup shredded American, cheddar, or Swiss cheese

2 scallions, chopped

Feel free to omit the cheese and scallion topping and replace with your preferred filling instead.

1 Put the flours and xantham gum into a bowl and make a well in the center, then gradually add the olive oil and measured water, stirring continuously, until it forms a fairly thick batter. Stir in the cilantro, chile, if using, and garlic.

2 Heat a little oil in a nonstick skillet, pour in one-quarter of the batter, and tilt the pan to form a thin layer. Cook for about 1 minute, until golden, then turn the pancake over and cook on the other side until golden.

3 Sprinkle with one-quarter of the cheese and scallions, then place under a preheated hot broiler and cook until the cheese has melted. Serve immediately.

4 Repeat with the remaining batter and ingredients to make the 3 remaining pancakes.

cheese & olive drop pancakes

Serves 4

Preparation time 10 minutes

Cooking time 6–12 minutes

1 cup ricotta cheese

⅔ cup milk

3 eggs, separated

⅔ cup rice flour

1 teaspoon gluten-free baking powder

1 tablespoon chopped chives

12 pitted olives, quartered

½ cup shredded Gruyère or Swiss cheese

2 tablespoons grated Parmesan cheese

1 tablespoon butter

To serve (optional)

fried or broiled bacon slices

cherry tomatoes, halved

1 Beat together the ricotta, milk, and egg yolks in a large bowl. Sift together the flour and baking powder in a separate bowl, then fold into the ricotta mixture.

2 Whisk the egg whites in a clean bowl until they form stiff peaks, then fold into the ricotta mixture with the chives, olives, Gruyère or Swiss, and Parmesan.

3 Heat a little of the butter in a nonstick skillet, add spoonfuls of the batter, and cook for 1–2 minutes on each side. Transfer to a serving plate and keep warm while you cook the remaining batter, adding the remaining butter to the pan as necessary.

4 Serve warm with crispy bacon and halved cherry tomatoes, if desired.

veggie pastry pockets

Makes 4

Preparation time 15 minutes

Cooking time 50 minutes

1 leek, trimmed, cleaned, and finely sliced

1 potato, cut into small cubes

⅔ cup diced rutabaga, sweet potato, or carrots

1 cup shredded Jarlsberg or cheddar cheese

milk, for brushing

salt and black pepper

Pastry dough

2 cups rice flour, plus extra for dusting

½ teaspoon xanthan gum

¼ cup fine cornmeal

pinch of paprika (optional)

1¼ sticks cold butter, cubed

1 egg yolk

1 Make the pastry dough. Put the flour, xanthan gum, cornmeal, paprika, if using, and butter into a food processor and process until the mixture resembles fine bread crumbs. Alternatively, mix together the dry ingredients in a large bowl, then add the butter and rub in with the fingertips until the mixture resembles fine bread crumbs. Add the egg yolk and enough cold water to form a dough.

2 Meanwhile, mix together the vegetables and cheese in a bowl and season with salt and black pepper.

3 Turn the dough out on a surface lightly dusted with rice flour and divide into 4 equal pieces. Gently roll out each piece to a disk about 8 inches in diameter. Divide the vegetable mixture evenly among the disks of dough, then close up the edges and crimp together. Make a small slit in the top of each pastry pocket and brush with milk.

4 Transfer the pastry pockets to a baking sheet and place in a preheated oven, at 425°F, for 10 minutes, then reduce the heat to 350°F and cook for an additional 40 minutes, until golden.

Hints and tips

If you prefer smaller pastry pockets, divide the dough into 8 pieces and roll out to 6 inches in diameter. After the initial 10 minutes cooking, they will take only an additional 25–30 minutes to bake.

beef pastry pockets

Makes 4

Preparation time 15 minutes

Cooking time 50 minutes

8 oz skirt steak, cut into small pieces

1 onion, finely chopped

1 potato, cut into small cubes

⅔ cup diced rutabaga, sweet potato, or carrots

milk, for brushing

salt and black pepper

Pastry dough

2 cups rice flour, plus extra for dusting

½ teaspoon xanthan gum

¼ cup fine cornmeal

pinch of paprika (optional)

1¼ sticks cold butter, cubed

1 egg yolk

1 Make the pastry dough. Put the flour, xanthan gum, cornmeal, paprika, if using, and butter into a food processor and process until the mixture resembles fine bread crumbs. Alternatively, mix together the dry ingredients in a large bowl, then add the butter and rub in with the fingertips until the mixture resembles fine bread crumbs. Add the egg yolk and enough cold water to form a ball of dough.

2 Mix together the steak and vegetables in a bowl and season with salt and black pepper.

3 Turn out the dough onto a surface lightly dusted with rice flour and divide into 4 equal pieces. Gently roll each piece out to a disk about 8 inches in diameter. Divide the beef mixture evenly among the disks of dough, then close up the edges and crimp together. Make a small slit in the top of each pastry pocket and brush with milk.

4 Transfer the pastry pockets to a baking sheet and place in a preheated oven, at 425°F, for 10 minutes, then reduce the heat to 350°F and cook for an additional 40 minutes, until golden and cooked through.

Hints and tips

If you prefer smaller pastry pockets, divide the dough into 8 pieces and roll out to 6 inches in diameter. After the initial 10 minutes cooking, they will take only an additional 25–30 minutes to bake.

picnic eggs

Makes 12

Preparation time 15 minutes, plus chilling

Cooking time 15 minutes

12 quail eggs

3 cups gluten-free cornflakes

⅓ cup fine cornmeal

10 oz gluten-free sausage links, skins removed, or sausagemeat

1 tablespoon chopped parsley

1 tablespoon snipped chives

good grating of nutmeg

⅓ cup rice flour, plus extra for shaping into balls

2 eggs, beaten

4 cups oil, for deep-frying

salt and black pepper

These hard-boiled eggs surrounded in sausagemeat and coated in cornflakes are perfect little snacks or great for a picnic.

1 Place the quail eggs in a small saucepan, pour boiling water over them, bring to a boil, and cook for 2 minutes. Drain, then transfer to a bowl of ice cold water and let cool.

2 Meanwhile, put the cornflakes into a food processor and process to fine crumbs. Transfer to a shallow dish and stir in the cornmeal. Set aside.

3 Put the sausagemeat, herbs, and nutmeg into a bowl and mash together. Season well. Divide the mixture into 12 equal pieces, then roll into balls with floured hands and flatten slightly.

4 Shell the eggs, place each one in the center of a sausagemeat disk, and gently bring the edges together to encase them.

5 Put the rice flour onto a plate and the beaten eggs in shallow bowl. Roll each sausagemeat ball in the flour, then dip into the beaten egg and roll in the cornflake mixture. Transfer to a plate and chill for 30 minutes.

6 Fill a large saucepan halfway with oil and heat to 350–375°F, or until a cube of bread browns in 30 seconds. Deep-fry the coated eggs, in batches, for 5–6 minutes minutes, until golden and cooked through. Remove with a slotted spoon and retain for future use. Drain the eggs on paper towels and serve cool.

cheesy veggie biscuits

Makes 8

Preparation time 10 minutes

Cooking time 12–15 minutes

1 cup plus 2 tablespoons rice flour,
  plus extra for dusting

⅔ cup cornstarch

1 teaspoon gluten-free baking powder

1 teaspoon baking soda

6 tablespoons cold butter, cubed,
  plus extra to serve

⅔ cup chopped frozen leaf spinach, first
  defrosted and squeezed of any liquid

4 sun-dried tomatoes in oil, drained and
  finely chopped

½ cup grated Parmesan cheese

good grating of nutmeg

1 extra-large egg, beaten

3 tablespoons buttermilk, plus extra
  for brushing

1 Put the rice flour, cornstarch, baking powder, baking soda, and butter into a food processor and process until the mixture resembles fine bread crumbs. Alternatively, mix together the dry ingredients in a large bowl. Add the butter and rub in with the fingertips until the mixture resembles fine bread crumbs. Mix in the spinach, sun-dried tomatoes, Parmesan, and nutmeg.

2 Whisk together the egg and buttermilk in a separate bowl, stir in the flour mixture, and combine to form a soft dough.

3 Turn out the dough on a surface lightly dusted with rice flour, press out to 1 inch thick, and stamp out 8 biscuits using a 2 inch round cutter, rerolling the scraps as necessary.

4 Transfer to a baking sheet lightly dusted with rice flour, brush with a little buttermilk, and place in a preheated oven, at 425°F, for 12–15 minutes, until risen and golden. Serve warm, spread with butter.

falafel with zingy salsa

Makes 12

Preparation time 10 minutes, plus chilling

Cooking time 20 minutes

1 (14 oz) can chickpeas, rinsed and drained

1 small red onion, coarsely chopped

1 teaspoon ground cumin

1 teaspoon ground coriander

1 teaspoon chili powder

2 garlic cloves, crushed

handful of fresh herbs, such as mint, cilantro, and parsley

1 tablespoon chickpea (besan) flour

a little oil, for brushing

For the salsa

2 large tomatoes, finely chopped

½ red onion, finely sliced

½ red chile, finely chopped

handful fresh cilantro

good squeeze fresh lime

1 Put all the ingredients except the oil into a food processor or blender and process until well combined but still retaining some texture.

2 Shape the mixture into 12 equal smallish balls and flatten slightly. Chill for about 20 minutes, until firm.

3 Transfer the falafel to a baking sheet and brush with a little oil. Place in a preheated oven, at 400°F, for 20 minutes, until crisp and golden.

4 Stir together the salsa and ingredients and serve with the falafel.

sesame pita breads

Makes 8

Preparation time 10 minutes, plus proving

Cooking time 10 minutes

2 cups chickpea (besan) flour

2 cups rice flour, plus extra for dusting

2 teaspoons xanthan gum

⅓ cup sesame seeds

2 teaspoons baking powder

1 tablespoon sugar

3 tablespoons olive oil, plus extra for oiling

1¼ cups warm milk

1 Mix the dry ingredients in a large bowl. Whisk together the oil and milk and gradually pour into the dry ingredients to form a slightly sticky dough, adding a little more flour or liquid, if needed.

2 Turn out the dough on a surface lightly dusted with rice flour and knead for 5 minutes, until smooth. Put into a lightly oiled bowl, cover with a clean, damp dish towel, and let rest in a warm place for about 1 hour to rise a little.

3 Turn out the dough onto the floured surface and divide into 8 equal pieces. Roll each piece out to about ¼ inch thick and flatten into a pita shape.

4 Transfer the pitas to a wire rack, splash with a little water, and place in a preheated oven, at 425°F, for 8–10 minutes, until beginning to turn golden. Serve immediately.

red pepper hummus

Serves 4

Preparation time 5 minutes

1 (12 oz) jar red peppers in oil, drained

1 (15 oz) can chickpeas, drained

1 garlic clove, crushed

juice of ½ lemon

¼ cup plain yogurt

handful of fresh cilantro, chopped

pinch each of cayenne pepper and salt

1 Put all the ingredients into a food processor or blender and process together until blended.

2 Serve with pita breads (*see* above).

pita chips

Serves 8

Preparation time 5 minutes

Cooking time 8–10 minutes

8 gluten-free pita breads (for homemade, *see* opposite)

¼ cup olive oil

4 garlic cloves, finely sliced

large rosemary sprig, coarsely crumbled

sprinkling of sea salt

1 Cut the pitas into rough triangles. Drizzle with the oil, sprinkle with the garlic, rosemary, and sea salt, and toss to coat well.

2 Spread out the bread on a baking sheet and place in a preheated oven, at 400°F, for 8–10 minutes, turning occasionally, until crisp and golden.

cheesy dip

Serves 4

Preparation time 5 minutes

1 cup cream cheese

2 scallions, sliced

1 cup shredded cheddar cheese

a little milk

1 Beat together all the ingredients in a bowl, adding enough milk to make a good dipping consistency.

2 Serve with fresh carrot and cucumber sticks.

feta, mint & pea dip

Preparation time 5 minutes

Cooking time 3 minutes

6 mint leaves

2 cups frozen peas

1 cup feta cheese

¾ cup plain yogurt

1 Put the mint and peas into a saucepan of boiling water, bring back to a boil, then drain immediately and refresh under cold running water.

2 Transfer to a food processor or blender, add the feta and yogurt, and process together until combined but still retaining a little texture.

baked eggplant dip

Preparation time 10 minutes

Cooking time 35–45 minutes

2 eggplants

1 tablespoon olive oil

1 garlic clove, crushed

½ inch piece of fresh ginger root, peeled and grated

1 small green chile, seeded and finely chopped

2 scallions, finely chopped

1 teaspoon cumin seeds

½ teaspoon ground coriander

1 tablespoon chopped fresh cilantro

few mint leaves, chopped

2 tablespoons plain yogurt

salt

1 Prick the eggplants all over, put onto a baking sheet, and bake in a preheated oven, at 350°F, for 30–40 minutes, until tender.

2 Meanwhile, heat the oil in a large skillet, add the garlic, ginger, chile, and scallions, and sauté for 2 minutes. Add the cumin seeds and ground coriander and continue to sauté for 1 minute. Remove the pan from the heat.

3 Cut the eggplants in half and scrape out all the flesh, add to the pan, and cook for 5 minutes, until all the liquid has evaporated.

4 Transfer the mixture to a food processor or blender and process for a few seconds until almost smooth but still retaining a little texture. Stir in all the remaining ingredients and season with salt. Serve warm or at room temperature.

lazy day baked eggs

Serves 4

Preparation time 5 minutes

Cooking time 10 minutes

butter, for greasing

4 slices of ham or smoked salmon

4 eggs

¼ cup heavy cream

¼ cup shredded cheddar cheese

salt and black pepper

toast, to serve

So simple, yet wonderfully delicious. You can place a layer of whatever takes your fancy in the bottom of the ramekins—blanched asparagus is delicious.

1 Grease 4 ramekins with butter, then place 1 slice of ham or smoked salmon in the bottom of each ramekin and crack an egg into each one.

2 Pour 1 tablespoon of the cream over the top of each, then sprinkle with the cheese and season well.

3 Transfer the ramekins to a baking sheet and place in a preheated oven, at 400°F, for 10 minutes, until set. Serve with toast.

Hints and tips

This can be made into a more filling meal for grown-ups by adding two eggs and extra fillings to each ramekin.

dosa with spicy potatoes

Makes 8

Preparation time 20 minutes,
plus soaking and standing

Cooking time 30 minutes

1⅔ cups basmati or other long-grain rice

1 cup black lentils

½ teaspoon fenugreek seeds

a little oil, for frying

salt

Spicy potatoes

6 Yukon gold or red-skinned potatoes
(about 1½ lb), peeled and cut into
bite-size chunks

3 tablespoons sunflower oil

2 garlic cloves, crushed

½ inch piece of fresh ginger root,
peeled and grated

1 teaspoon mustard seeds

pinch of ground cumin

pinch of ground coriander

pinch of turmeric

Yogurt sauce

⅔ cup plain yogurt

handful of mint and fresh cilantro,
chopped

½ teaspoon sugar

½ green chile, seeded and chopped
(optional)

Although the dosa-making process takes time, the results are well worth it. Remember to start to make them the night before you want to serve them.

1 Rinse the rice and lentils, then drain and transfer to a large bowl. Cover with cold water and let soak overnight.

2 Drain the rice and lentils, transfer to a food processor or blender, and process until smooth, adding enough water to make a smooth batter. Season with salt, cover, and let stand for 6 hours.

3 Cook the potatoes in a saucepan of lightly salted boiling water for about 10 minutes, until just tender. Drain.

4 Heat the sunflower oil in a large skillet, add the garlic, ginger, mustard seeds, and spices, and sauté for 1 minute, then add to the potatoes, toss with the spice mixture, and cook over low heat for 5–6 minutes. Keep warm.

5 Mix together all the yogurt sauce ingredients in a bowl. Set aside.

6 Heat a little oil in a heavy, nonstick skillet, add 1 tablespoon of the dosa batter to the pan, and spread out thinly. Cook for 1 minute, then turn the dosa over and cook for an additional 20 seconds. Remove from the pan and keep warm while you cook the remaining batter.

7 Wrap the potatoes in the dosa and serve with the yogurt sauce for spooning over the top.

crunchy sweet potato bites

Serves 4

Preparation time 10 minutes

Cooking time 30–40 minutes

2 large sweet potatoes, ends removed
and each potato cut into 6 thick slices

a little oil, for brushing

⅔ cup crumbled feta cheese

⅔ cup finely chopped mozzarella cheese

2 crispy, cooked bacon slices, crumbled

2 scallions, finely chopped

½ red or green chile, seeded
and finely chopped

The sweet potatoes can be replaced with ordinary potatoes, if you prefer, and the toppings can be varied with whatever you have on hand. Try quartered cherry tomatoes instead of bacon for a veggie version.

1 Cook the sweet potato slices in a saucepan of boiling water for 12–15 minutes, until just tender. Drain.

2 Place the slices on a baking sheet and brush both sides with a little oil. Bake in a preheated oven, at 400°F, for 10–15 minutes, until beginning to crisp.

3 Mix together all the remaining ingredients in a bowl, then spoon the topping over the potato slices. Return to the oven and cook for an additional 10 minutes, until golden and bubbling.

zucchini, corn & mozzarella fritters

Makes 12

Preparation time 10 minutes,
   plus standing

Cooking time 10 minutes

2 zucchini, grated

1¼ cups drained canned corn kernels

3 scallions, finely sliced

2 eggs, beaten

2 tablespoons chickpea (besan) flour

1 teaspoon gluten-free baking powder

5 oz mozzarella cheese, diced

2 tablespoons grated Parmesan cheese

⅓ cup olive oil

salt and black pepper

These veggie fritters are delicious served with Feta, Mint & Pea Dip (*see* page 48).

1 Sprinkle the zucchini with salt and let drain for about 20 minutes. Squeeze well, then transfer to a bowl, add all the remaining ingredients except the oil, and mix until combined.

2 Heat the oil in a large skillet, drop tablespoons of the fritter batter into the pan, in batches if necessary, and cook for 1–2 minutes on each side, until golden. Remove with a slotted spoon and drain on paper towels.

rice noodle salad

Serves 4

Preparation time 5 minutes, plus cooling

Cooking time about 5 minutes

8 oz rice noodles

2 cups shredded cooked chicken

1 large carrot, peeled and grated

¼ cup finely sliced snow peas

¾ cup bean sprouts

handful of mint and fresh cilantro, chopped

Dressing

2 tablespoons peanut butter

1 teaspoon gluten-free soy sauce

juice of ½ lime

1 tablespoon sweet chili sauce

A wonderful benefit provided by rice noodles is that they are a great gluten-free belly filler.

1 Cook the rice noodles according to the package directions, then drain and let cool.

2 Whisk together the dressing ingredients with 2 tablespoons of water in a small bowl.

3 Put the noodles, chicken, vegetables, and herbs into a large bowl and toss together. Pour the dressing over the noodles and combine until well coated.

Hints and tips

You can use the basis of the salad and add what you like to it—for example, shrimp or shredded duck instead of the chicken. You can also vary the veggies, adding zucchini or baby corn—just about anything will work.

harissa-spiced chicken drumsticks

Makes 8

Preparation time 5 minutes,
  plus marinating

Cooking time 10 minutes

8 chicken drumsticks, skin removed

2 tablespoons rose harissa

⅓ cup Greek yogurt

1 tablespoon olive oil

The drumsticks are delicious served with salad and pita breads, but they are also great served cold for a picnic. If you prefer, replace the harissa with a mild Indian curry paste, then prepare and cook in the same way.

1 Make 3 deep slashes in each drumstick and put into a nonmetallic bowl.

2 Mix together the harissa, yogurt, and oil in a separate bowl, then rub the mixture over the drumsticks. Cover with plastic wrap and let marinate in the refrigerator for at least 30 minutes.

3 Transfer the drumsticks to a baking sheet and cook under a preheated hot broiler for 8–10 minutes, turning occasionally, until cooked through.

ricotta & spinach tart

Serves 4

Preparation time 15 minutes, plus chilling

Cooking time 30 minutes

1 teaspoon olive oil

1 shallot, finely chopped

1 garlic clove, crushed

6 cups baby leaf spinach

1¼ cups ricotta cheese

½ cup light crème fraîche or sour cream

4 tablespoons grated Parmesan cheese

2 eggs, lightly beaten

grating of nutmeg

salt and black pepper

Pastry dough

1 cup rice flour, plus extra for dusting

⅔ cup cornmeal

1 stick cold butter, cubed

¼ cup grated Parmesan cheese

1 egg yolk

2 tablespoons milk

1 Make the pastry dough. Put the flour, cornmeal, butter, and Parmesan into a food processor and process until the mixture resembles fine bread crumbs. Alternatively, mix together the rice flour and cornmeal in a bowl. Add the butter and rub in with fingertips until the mixture resembles fine bread crumbs. Stir in the Parmesan. Mix together the egg yolk and milk in a separate bowl and add enough to the dry ingredients to form a soft but not sticky dough. Wrap in plastic wrap and chill for 30 minutes.

2 Roll out the dough on a surface lightly dusted with rice flour and use to line an 8 inch fluted tart pan. Prick the bottom of the shell with a fork and place in a preheated oven, at 400°F, for 10 minutes. Remove from the oven.

3 Meanwhile, heat the oil in a skillet, add the shallot and garlic, and sauté for 2–3 minutes, until softened. Add the spinach and cook for 3–4 minutes, until wilted and any moisture has evaporated.

4 Beat together the ricotta, crème fraîche or sour cream, half the Parmesan, and the eggs in a bowl, then season well with nutmeg and salt and black pepper. Stir in the spinach and pour into the tart shell, sprinkle with the remaining Parmesan, and return to the oven for 20 minutes, until firm and golden.

dinners

chicken & leek gratin

Serves 4

Preparation time 15 minutes

Cooking time 40–45 minutes

1 tablespoon olive oil

1 onion, chopped

1 garlic clove, crushed

4 leeks, trimmed, cleaned, and chopped

4 boneless, skinless chicken breasts
  (about 4 oz each), cut into chunks

½ cup dry white wine

1 tablespoon rice flour

1¼ cups gluten-free chicken broth

⅔ cup heavy cream

2 tablespoons chopped tarragon

1 tablespoon gluten-free English mustard

4 cups fresh gluten-free bread crumbs

1 cup shredded Gruyère or
  cheddar cheese

salt and black pepper

steamed vegetables, to serve

1 Heat the oil in a large saucepan, add the onion, garlic, and leeks, and sauté for 3–4 minutes. Transfer the vegetables to a plate, add the chicken to the pan, and cook for 3 minutes, until beginning to brown all over.

2 Add the wine and simmer until reduced by half. Add the flour and cook, stirring, for 1 minute, then gradually add the broth and cook, stirring continuously, until the sauce has thickened.

3 Stir in the leek mixture, cream, tarragon, and mustard and season well. Transfer to an ovenproof dish, then sprinkle with the bread crumbs and cheese.

4 Place in a preheated oven, at 400°F, for 25–30 minutes, until golden and bubbling. Serve with steamed vegetables.

ham, leek & potato gratin

Serves 4

Preparation time 15 minutes

Cooking time about 1 hour

butter, for greasing

6 red-skinned potatoes (about 1½ lb),
  thinly sliced

1 large leek, trimmed, cleaned,
  and thinly sliced

5 oz cured ham, chopped

2 tablespoons grated Parmesan cheese

⅔ cup heavy cream

⅔ cup gluten-free chicken or
  vegetable broth

1½ cups shredded sharp cheddar cheese

1 cup gluten-free fresh bread crumbs

salt and black pepper

1 Lightly butter a medium ovenproof dish or 4 individual dishes.

2 Arrange a layer of potatoes in the bottom of the dish, followed by a layer of leek and ham, then a sprinkling of Parmesan. Season well. Repeat the layers and seasoning, finishing with a layer of potatoes.

3 Stir together the cream and broth in a small bowl, then pour into the dish. Cover the dish with aluminum foil and place in a preheated oven, at 350°F, for 30 minutes.

4 Mix together the cheddar and bread crumbs in a bowl. Remove the foil from the dish and sprinkle the crumbs over the potato mixture. Return to the oven and bake for an additional 30–35 minutes or until golden and the potatoes are tender.

Hints and tips
This also works well as a side dish to serve loads of people if you are feeding a crowd.

lamb & apricot meatballs with fruity salsa

Serves 4

Preparation time 10 minutes

Cooking time 10 minutes

1 pound ground lamb

1 garlic clove, crushed

1 teaspoon ground cumin

1 teaspoon ground coriander

few dried red pepper flakes (optional)

3 tablespoons pine nuts, toasted

½ cup finely chopped dried apricots

gluten-free Pita Breads (*see* page 46)
  or steamed rice, to serve

Fruity salsa

½ mango, peeled and cut into
  small chunks

1 tablespoon chopped mint

1 tablespoon chopped fresh cilantro

¼ cucumber, finely chopped

juice of ½ lime

1 Put the lamb, garlic, spices, pine nuts, and apricots into a bowl and mix together until well combined. Shape the mixture into 20 equal balls.

2 Place the meatballs on a baking pan and cook under a preheated medium broiler for 6–7 minutes, turning occasionally, until browned and cooked through.

3 Meanwhile, mix together all the salsa ingredients in a bowl.

4 Serve the meatballs with the salsa and pita breads or rice.

fruity pork with butternut squash

Serves 4

Preparation time 5 minutes

Cooking time 20 minutes

½ butternut squash, peeled and cut into small chunks

1 cup trimmed and halved green beans

1 small onion, finely chopped

12 oz ground pork or turkey

1 (14½ oz) can diced tomatoes

2 tablespoons tomato paste

⅔ cup chopped dried apricots

1 tablespoon chopped mixed fresh herbs, such as cilantro, mint, and parsley

½ cup gluten-free chicken broth

black pepper

salt

steamed rice, to serve

1 Cook the squash and beans in a small saucepan of boiling water for 5 minutes. Drain.

2 Meanwhile, dry-fry the onion and meat in a nonstick saucepan for 4–5 minutes, until the meat is browned.

3 Add all the remaining ingredients to the saucepan with the squash and beans and bring to a boil. Reduce the heat and simmer for 20 minutes. Season well with balck pepper and serve with steamed rice.

lamb casserole with sweet potato topping

Serves 4

Preparation time 10 minutes

Cooking time 50–55 minutes

1 tablespoon olive oil

1 onion, chopped

1 garlic clove, crushed

1¼ lb ground lamb

1 teaspoon ground cumin

1 teaspoon ground coriander

pinch of ground cinnamon

1 (14½ oz) can diced tomatoes

1 tablespoon tomato paste

⅔ cup gluten-free beef or
   vegetable broth

Topping

4–5 sweet potatoes (about 1½ lb),
   peeled and chopped

1 tablespoon chopped fresh cilantro

⅓ cup Greek yogurt

1 tablespoon butter

salt and black pepper

1 Heat the oil in a large saucepan, add the onion and garlic, and sauté for 2–3 minutes, until softened. Add the meat and cook until browned, then add the spices and cook for an additional 1 minute.

2 Add the tomatoes, paste, and broth and bring to a boil, then reduce the heat, cover, and simmer for 45 minutes, until thickened slightly and the meat is tender.

3 Meanwhile, cook the sweet potatoes in a saucepan of lightly salted boiling water for 15–20 minutes, until tender. Drain, then season well and mash together with the cilantro, Greek yogurt, and butter.

4 Transfer the lamb mixture to a medium casserole dish or Dutch oven and spoon the mashed sweet potatoes over it. Cook under a preheated hot broiler for 2–3 minutes, until golden and bubbling.

beef pies with pesto pastry

Serves 4

Preparation time 15 minutes, plus chilling

Cooking time 2½–3 hours

2 tablespoons cornstarch

1½ lb lean boneless beef chuck or round, cubed

2 tablespoons sunflower oil

1 large onion, sliced

1 large carrot, peeled and chopped

1 thyme sprig

2 cups gluten-free beef broth

milk, for brushing

salt and black pepper

Pastry dough

1⅓ cups rice flour

3 tablespoons fine cornmeal

pinch of paprika (optional)

1 stick cold butter, cubed

1 tablespoon pesto

1 egg yolk

1 egg, beaten, to brush

Serve these pies with loads of veggies.

1 Place the cornstarch on a plate and season with salt and black pepper. Add the beef pieces and toss in the flour until coated.

2 Heat half the oil in a heavy flameproof casserole, add the onion, carrot, and thyme, and sauté for 3–4 minutes, until the vegetables begin to soften. Remove from the pan and set aside.

3 Add the beef to the pan and brown on all sides. Return the vegetables to the pan and stir in the broth. Bring to a boil, then reduce the heat, cover, and simmer for 1½–2 hours or until the meat is tender.

4 Meanwhile, make the pastry dough. Put flour, cornmeal, paprika, and butter into a food processor and process until the mixture resembles fine bread crumbs. Alternatively, mix together the dry ingredients in a large bowl. Add the butter and rub in with the fingertips until the mixture resembles fine bread crumbs. Beat together the pesto and egg yolk in a separate bowl and stir into the flour mixture with enough cold water to form a dough.

5 Fill 4 individual deep pie plates with the beef mixture. Roll out the dough between 2 sheets of plastic wrap to ¼ inch thick, then cut out disks big enough to cover your particular pie plates. Moisten the edges of the pie plates and use the dough disks to top the pie plates. Brush the tops with a little egg, then place in a preheated oven, at 350°F, for 35–40 minutes, until the pastry is cooked through and golden.

eggplant parmigiana

Serves 4

Preparation time 10 minutes

Cooking time 40–45 minutes

2 extra-large eggplants, sliced

2 tablespoons olive oil

5 oz mozzarella cheese, coarsely chopped

¼ cup grated Parmesan cheese

salt and black pepper

Tomato sauce

1 tablespoon olive oil

1 garlic clove, crushed

1 small onion, finely chopped

1 (14½ oz) can plum tomatoes

handful of basil, torn

To serve

salad

crusty gluten-free bread

1 Make the tomato sauce. Heat the oil in a saucepan, add the garlic and onion, and sauté for 3–4 minutes, until softened. Add the tomatoes and basil and bring to a boil, then reduce the heat and simmer for 15 minutes.

2 Meanwhile, brush the eggplant slices on each side with the oil. Heat a ridged grill pan until hot and cook the eggplant slices for 1–2 minutes on each side, until tender and browned.

3 Spoon a little of the tomato sauce into an ovenproof dish, layer over half the eggplants, sprinkle with half the mozzarella and Parmesan, and season well. Repeat the layering with the remaining ingredients, finishing with a sprinkling of the cheeses.

4 Place in a preheated oven, at 400°F, for 20–25 minutes, until golden. Serve with salad and crusty bread.

potato pizza margherita

Serves 3–4

Preparation time 20 minutes, plus cooling

Cooking time 45 minutes

8 russet potatoes (about 2 lb), peeled and cut into small chunks

3 tablespoons olive oil, plus extra for oiling

1 egg, beaten

½ cup grated Parmesan or cheddar cheese

¼ cup gluten-free tomato paste or ketchup

4–5 small tomatoes (about 1 lb), thinly sliced

4 oz mozzarella cheese, thinly sliced

1 tablespoon chopped thyme, plus extra sprigs to garnish (optional)

salt

1 Boil the potatoes in salted water for 15 minutes or until tender. Drain well, return to the pan, and cool for 10 minutes.

2 Add 2 tablespoons of the oil, the egg, and half the cheese to the potatoes and mix well. Turn out onto an oiled baking sheet and spread out to form a 10 inch disk. Place in a preheated oven, at 400°F, for 15 minutes.

3 Remove from the oven and spread with the tomato paste or ketchup. Arrange the tomato and mozzarella slices on top. Sprinkle with the remaining grated Parmesan, thyme, if using, and a little salt. Drizzle with the remaining oil.

4 Return to the oven for an additional 15 minutes, until the potatoes are crisp around the edges and the cheese is melting. Cut into wedges, garnish with thyme sprigs, if desired, and serve.

golden buttermilk chicken & zingy coleslaw

Serves 6

Preparation time 10 minutes,
plus marinating

Cooking time 25–30 minutes

12 chicken drumsticks or boneless
chicken thighs

⅔ cup buttermilk

good pinch of cayenne pepper

½ cup rice flour

½ cup chickpea (besan) flour

pinch of chili powder

pinch of dried oregano

¼ cup sunflower oil, for frying

salt

Coleslaw

½ red or green cabbage, finely sliced

1 large carrot, peeled and cut into ribbons

2 scallions, finely sliced

juice of 1 lime

⅔ cup plain yogurt

1 Put the chicken pieces into a nonmetallic bowl. Stir together the buttermilk and cayenne in a separate bowl and season well. Pour the buttermilk over the chicken and toss well to coat, then cover and let marinate in the refrigerator for at least 1 hour, but preferably overnight.

2 Mix together the flours, chili powder, and oregano in a bowl and pour onto a plate. Remove the chicken from the marinade, draining off any excess buttermilk, then dust the pieces well with the flour mixture.

3 Heat the oil in a large, deep skillet to 350–375°F, or until a cube of bread browns in 30 seconds. Cook the chicken for 3–4 minutes on each side, until golden, then transfer to a baking sheet. Place in a preheated oven, at 425°F, for 20 minutes or until cooked through.

4 Make the coleslaw. Put all the ingredients into a serving bowl and toss together, then serve with the chicken.

spaghetti & vegetable sauce

Serves 2

Preparation time 10 minutes

Cooking time 40–50 minutes

1 tablespoon vegetable oil

1 onion, finely chopped

1 garlic clove, finely chopped

1 celery stick, finely chopped

1 carrot, peeled and finely chopped

1 cup coarsely chopped cremini
 mushrooms

1 tablespoon tomato paste

1 (14½ oz) can diced tomatoes

1 cup red wine or gluten-free
 vegetable broth

pinch of dried mixed herbs

1 teaspoon yeast extract

1½ cups textured vegetable protein

2 tablespoons chopped parsley

8 oz gluten-free spaghetti

salt and black pepper

grated Parmesan cheese, to serve

1 Heat the oil in a large, heavy saucepan over medium heat. Add the onion, garlic, celery, carrot, and mushrooms and cook, stirring frequently, for 5 minutes or until softened. Add the tomato paste and cook, stirring, for an additional minute.

2 Add the tomatoes, wine or broth, herbs, yeast extract, and textured vegetable protein. Bring to a boil, then reduce the heat, cover, and simmer for 30–40 minutes, until the vegetable protein is tender. Stir in the parsley and season well.

3 Meanwhile, cook the pasta in a large saucepan of salted boiling water according to the package directions until al dente. Drain well.

4 Divide the pasta between 2 serving plates, top with the vegetable mixture, and serve immediately with a sprinkling of grated Parmesan.

sausage & pea pasta

Serves 4

Preparation time 5 minutes

Cooking time about 10 minutes

1 tablespoon olive oil

6 gluten-free sausage links, chopped

½ gluten-free chicken or vegetable
  bouillon cube

¼ cup boiling water

2 teaspoons gluten-free Dijon mustard

⅔ cup heavy cream or light crème fraîche

12 oz gluten-free pasta

1⅓ cups frozen peas

1 Heat the oil in large skillet, add the sausages, and cook for 4–5 minutes, until browned all over.

2 Crumble in the bouillon cube and add the measured water. Simmer and scrape all the sediment from the bottom of the pan. Stir in the mustard and cream or crème fraîche and simmer for an additional few minutes.

3 Meanwhile, cook the pasta in a saucepan of boiling water according to the package directions until tender, adding the peas 2 minutes before the end of the cooking time. Drain and return to the pan, then toss through the sausage mixture and serve.

hazelnut, parsley & basil pesto

Serves 4

Preparation time 5 minutes

Cooking time about 10 minutes

1¼ cups hazelnuts, toasted

1 garlic clove, crushed

handful each of parsley and basil leaves

1 cup grated Parmesan cheese

good pinch of red pepper flakes (optional)

½ cup light olive oil

12 oz gluten-free fusilli

1 Put all the ingredients into a food processor or blender and process until blended but still retaining a little texture.

2 Cook the fusilli in a saucepan of boiling water according to the package directions until tender. Stir through the pesto and serve immediately.

spicy chorizo & tomato sauce

Serves 4

Preparation time 5 minutes

Cooking time 15 minutes

5 oz chorizo, chopped

1 garlic clove, crushed

1 (14½ oz) can plum tomatoes, processed in a food processor or blender until smooth, or 1¾ cups tomato puree or tomato sauce

handful of basil, coarsely chopped

pinch of sugar

12 oz gluten-free penne

grated Parmesan cheese, to serve

1 Dry-fry the chorizo in a medium saucepan over medium heat until beginning to brown. Add all the remaining ingredients, except the pasta, and bring to a boil, then reduce the heat and simmer gently for 10 minutes.

2 Cook the penne in a saucepan of boiling water according to the package directions until tender. Stir through the sauce and serve sprinkled with Parmesan.

zucchini & mascarpone sauce

Serves 4

Preparation time 5 minutes

Cooking time 10–15 minutes

1 tablespoon olive oil

1 garlic clove, crushed

2 zucchini, coarsely grated

grated zest of 1 lemon

¼ cup mascarpone cheese

2 tablespoons grated Parmesan cheese

⅓ cup pine nuts, toasted

12 oz gluten-free pasta

1 Heat the oil in a skillet, add the garlic, zucchini, and lemon zest, and sauté gently for 3–4 minutes, until softened.

2 Meanwhile, cook the pasta in a saucepan of boiling water according to the package directions until tender.

3 Toss the sauce through the pasta and stir in the mascarpone and Parmesan. Sprinkle the pine nuts over the top and serve.

bacon & spinach pasta

Serves 4

Preparation time 10 minutes

Cooking time 10–15 minutes

12 oz gluten-free pasta

1 tablespoon olive oil

8 oz bacon slices

1 onion, sliced

2 tablespoons pine nuts

6 cups baby leaf spinach

2 cups halved cherry tomatoes

⅓ cup light cream

2 tablespoons grated Parmesan cheese

4 scallions, sliced

salt and black pepper

1 Cook the pasta in a saucepan of salted boiling water according to the package directions until tender.

2 Meanwhile, heat the oil in a skillet, add the bacon and onion, and sauté for 3–4 minutes, until the bacon is crisp and the onion softened.

3 Add the pine nuts and cook for 1 minute. Stir in the spinach and tomatoes and cook until the spinach is just wilted.

4 Drain the pasta and return to the pan, then stir in the spinach mixture. Mix in the cream, Parmesan, and scallions, season well, and serve immediately.

chicken & spinach curry

Serves 4

Preparation time 5 minutes

Cooking time about 20 minutes

1 tablespoon vegetable oil

4 boneless, skinless chicken breasts
  (about 4 oz each), halved lengthwise

1 onion, sliced

2 garlic cloves, chopped

1 green chile, seeded and chopped

4 cardamom pods

1 teaspoon cumin seeds

1 teaspoon red pepper flakes

1 teaspoon ground coriander

1 teaspoon turmeric

1 tablespoon mild curry powder

8 cups baby leaf spinach

3 tomatoes, chopped

⅔ cup light Greek yogurt

2 tablespoons chopped fresh cilantro

steamed rice, to serve

1 Heat the oil in large, nonstick saucepan or skillet, add the chicken, onion, and garlic, and sauté for 4–5 minutes, until the chicken is beginning to brown and the onion softens. Stir in the chile, cardamom, cumin, red pepper flakes, ground coriander, turmeric, and curry powder and sauté for an additional 1 minute.

2 Add the spinach and cook gently until wilted, then stir in the tomatoes, cover, and simmer for 15 minutes, removing the lid for the final 5 minutes of cooking time.

3 Stir in the yogurt and cilantro and serve with steamed rice.

Hints and tips

If you prefer to eat your curry with bread, try the gluten-free pita breads on page 46, or wrapped in the dosas on page 50.

fancy baked beans with poached eggs

Serves 4

Preparation time 5 minutes

Cooking time 25 minutes

1 tablespoon sunflower oil

1 onion, chopped

1 garlic clove, crushed

3 oz bacon or chorizo, chopped

1 (14½ oz) can diced tomatoes

1 tablespoon tomato paste

2 (15 oz) cans cannellini (white kidney) beans, rinsed and drained

½ teaspoon sugar

1 tablespoon white wine vinegar

4 eggs

These baked beans are delicious served with toasted Cheesy Bread (*see* page 113). If you prefer a vegetarian option, omit the bacon or chorizo.

1 Heat the oil in a medium skillet, add the onion and garlic, and sauté gently for 2–3 minutes, until softened. Add all the remaining ingredients except the eggs, cover, and simmer for 20 minutes, until thickened slightly.

2 Make 4 wells in the tomato mixture and crack an egg into each, put the lid back on, and cook for 2–3 minutes, until the eggs are just cooked through.

baked vegetables & lentils

Serves 4

Preparation time 10 minutes

Cooking time 50 minutes

1 red bell pepper, cored, seeded,
  and sliced

2 zucchini, halved lengthwise and
  cut into chunks

1 large sweet potato, peeled and cut
  into chunks

1 red onion, cut into wedges

1 tablespoon olive oil

¾ cup red lentils

3 cups gluten-free vegetable broth

1 cup crumbled feta cheese

4 oz mozzarella cheese, chopped

2 tablespoons grated Parmesan cheese

1 Put the red bell pepper, zucchini, sweet potato, and onion into a large roasting pan and drizzle with the oil. Place in a preheated oven, at 425°F, for 25–30 minutes, until charred and softened.

2 Remove from the oven and sprinkle with the lentils, then pour the broth over the top. Return to the oven and bake for an additional 15 minutes, until the lentils are tender.

3 Mix together the cheeses in a bowl, then sprinkle them over the vegetables and cook for an additional 2–3 minutes, until melted.

battered fish with pea puree

Serves 4

Preparation time 10 minutes

Cooking time 5 minutes

oil, for deep-frying

1 cup chickpea (besan) flour,
  plus extra for coating

⅔ cup ice-cold sparkling water

4 small white fish fillets (about 4 oz each),
  such as cod or halibut

salt and black pepper

Pea puree

2½ cups frozen peas

1 small onion, finely chopped

1¼ cups boiling gluten-free
  vegetable broth

¼ cup heavy cream

Serve this the traditional way, with fries.

1 Fill a deep skillet halfway with oil and heat to 350–375°F, or until a cube of bread browns in 30 seconds.

2 Meanwhile, put the flour into a large bowl and season well. Pour in the sparkling water and whisk to combine. Dredge the fish fillets with flour, then dip into the batter.

3 Deep-fry the fish in the hot oil for 3–4 minutes, turning occasionally, until golden on all sides and cooked through.

4 Meanwhile, put the peas, onion, and broth into a saucepan and simmer for 3 minutes. Drain, then transfer to a food processor or blender, add the cream, and process to a puree. Season and serve with the battered fish.

salmon & pea risotto

Serves 4

Preparation time 5 minutes

Cooking time 25 minutes

1 teaspoon olive oil

1 small onion, finely chopped

2 cups risotto rice

5 cups boiling gluten-free vegetable broth

9 oz skinless salmon fillet, cubed

1⅓ cups frozen peas, defrosted

2 tablespoons chopped parsley

3 tablespoons grated Parmesan cheese

arugula and tomato salad, to serve

1 Heat the oil in a large nonstick skillet, add the onion, and sauté for 2–3 minutes, until beginning to soften. Add the rice and stir well to coat in the oil.

2 Add the broth, a ladleful at a time, stirring continuously, until the liquid has been absorbed and the rice is just tender—this should take about 20 minutes.

3 Add the salmon and peas with the final ladleful of broth and cook until the fish is just cooked through and the peas are tender. Stir in the parsley and Parmesan.

4 Serve the risotto with arugula and tomato salad.

sweet potatoes with tomato salsa

Serves 4

Preparation time 10 minutes

Cooking time 45 minutes

4 large sweet potatoes (about 8 oz each)

2 tablespoons olive oil

1 cup shredded Monterey Jack, Gruyère, or cheddar cheese

salt

green salad, to serve

Salsa

4 large tomatoes, finely chopped

1 small red onion, finely chopped

2 celery sticks, finely chopped

handful of fresh cilantro, chopped

¼ cup lime juice

4 teaspoons sugar

1 Scrub the potatoes and put them into a small roasting pan. Prick with a fork, drizzle with the oil, and sprinkle with a little salt. Place in a preheated oven, at 400°F, for 45 minutes, until tender.

2 Meanwhile, make the salsa. Mix together the tomatoes, onion, celery, cilantro, lime juice, and sugar in a bowl.

3 Halve the potatoes and fluff up the flesh with a fork. Sprinkle with the cheese and top with the salsa. Serve with a green salad.

cauliflower & broccoli gratin

Serves 4

Preparation time 10 minutes

Cooking time 20 minutes

8 bacon slices

4 tablespoons butter

1 cauliflower, cut into florets

1 head of broccoli, cut into florets

3 tablespoons cornstarch

1¼ cups milk

1 cup shredded Gruyère, cheddar,
  or American cheese

1 cup gluten-free fresh bread crumbs

salt and black pepper

1 Cook the bacon under a medium broiler or in skillet over medium heat, turning once, until cooked through and crisp.

2 Meanwhile, heat half the butter in a skillet, add the cauliflower and broccoli, and sauté until just tender. Transfer to an ovenproof dish.

3 Melt the remaining butter in a saucepan, add the cornstarch, and cook, stirring, for 1 minute. Gradually add the milk and cook, stirring continuously, until thickened and smooth, then season well. Stir in two-thirds of the cheese, then crumble in half the cooked bacon.

4 Pour the sauce over the vegetables. Mix together the remaining cheese and the bread crumbs and sprinkle the mixture over the top with the remaining bacon.

5 Place in a preheated oven, at 400°F, for 10–12 minutes, until golden and bubbling.

crab cakes

Serves 4

Preparation time 15 minutes, plus cooling and chilling

Cooking time 20 minutes

3 russet potatoes, peeled and chopped

12 oz fresh white crab meat

3 scallions, sliced

handful of fresh cilantro, leaves and stems finely chopped

good squeeze of lime juice

½ chile, seeded and finely chopped

1 egg yolk

3 tablespoons cornmeal

2 tablespoons vegetable oil

salt and black pepper

To serve

gluten-free chili dipping sauce

lime wedges

mixed green salad

1 Cook the potatoes in a saucepan of salted boiling water for 15 minutes or until tender. Drain well, return to the pan, and mash. Let cool. Stir in all the remaining ingredients except the cornmeal and oil.

2 Put the cornmeal onto a plate, shape the crab mixture into 8 cakes, and coat in the cornmeal. Cover with plastic wrap and chill for 20 minutes.

3 Heat the oil in a large skillet, add the cakes, and cook for 2–3 minutes on each side, until golden.

4 Serve with a mixed green salad, gluten-free chili dipping sauce, and lime wedges.

baked spinach & fish

Serves 4

Preparation time 15 minutes

Cooking time 45–55 minutes

1 tablespoon olive oil

1 onion, chopped

6 cups baby leaf spinach

4 tablespoons butter

2½ tablespoons rice flour

2½ cups milk

1 tablespoon gluten-free whole-grain
  mustard

good grating of nutmeg

1½ lb mixed skinless salmon, halibut, and
  red snapper fillets, cut into chunks

8 oz shrimp, peeled and deveined

salt and black pepper

Potato topping

8 russet potatoes (about 2 lb),
  peeled and cut into chunks

pat of butter

½ cup light cream

1 Make the potato topping. Cook the potatoes in a saucepan of salted boiling water for 15 minutes or until tender. Drain well and return to the pan. Mash together with the butter and cream and season well.

2 Heat the oil in a large saucepan, add the onion, and sauté for 2–3 minutes, until beginning to soften. Add the spinach to the pan and cook until wilted and any liquid has evaporated.

3 Melt the butter in a saucepan, add the flour, and cook, stirring, for 1 minute. Gradually add the milk and cook, stirring continuously, until thickened and smooth. Stir in the mustard and nutmeg and season well.

4 Arrange the fish and the shrimp in a large ovenproof dish and top with the spinach. Pour over the sauce, spoon the mashed potatoes on top, and place in a preheated oven, at 400°F, for 30–35 minutes, until golden and bubbling.

baked goods
& desserts

carrot & orange muffins

Makes 12

Preparation time 10 minutes

Cooking time 15–18 minutes

¾ cup superfine or granulated sugar

1 cup rice flour

¾ cup cornstarch

1 tablespoon gluten-free baking powder

1 carrot, peeled and grated

2 tablespoons buttermilk

1¼ sticks butter, melted

3 eggs, beaten

grated zest of 2 oranges

1 cup confectioners' sugar

1 Line a 12-cup muffin pan with paper muffin cups.

2 Mix together the sugar, flour, cornstarch, baking powder, and carrot in a bowl. Whisk together the buttermilk, butter, eggs, and orange zest in a separate bowl, then pour into the dry ingredients and stir until just combined.

3 Spoon the batter into the muffin cups and place in a preheated oven, at 350°F, for 15–18 minutes, until golden and springy to the touch. Let cool.

4 Sift the confectioners' sugar into a bowl. Add a tablespoon warm water and stir until the icing is thick enough to coat the spoon, adding extra drops of water as necessary. Drizzle the icing over the muffins and let set.

cherry crumble muffins

Makes 12

Preparation time 10 minutes

Cooking time 20 minutes

1½ cups brown rice flour

1 teaspoon baking soda

2 teaspoons gluten-free baking powder

⅔ cup superfine or granulated sugar

1⅔ cups drained canned black cherries

6 tablespoons butter, melted

2 eggs, beaten

⅔ cup buttermilk

Topping

1 tablespoon ground almonds
  (almond meal)

1 tablespoon packed light brown sugar

1 tablespoon brown rice flour

1 tablespoons butter

1 Line a 12-cup muffin pan with paper muffin cups.

2 Sift the flour, baking soda, and baking powder into a large bowl, then stir in the sugar. Mix together the cherries, melted butter, eggs, and buttermilk in a separate bowl, then pour into the dry ingredients and stir gently until just combined. Spoon the batter into the muffin cups.

3 Put the topping ingredients into a food processor and process until the mixture resembles fine bread crumbs. Alternatively, mix together the ground almonds, sugar, and flour in a bowl. Add the butter and rub in with the finegrtips until the mixture resembles fine bread crumbs. Sprinkle the topping over the muffin mixture.

4 Place in a preheated oven, at 350°F, for 20 minutes, until golden and firm to the touch. Transfer to a wire rack to cool.

apricot & saffron muffins

Makes 12

Preparation time 10 minutes, plus cooling

Cooking time 25 minutes

¾ cup coarsely chopped dried apricots

grated zest and juice of 1 orange

pinch of saffron threads

1⅓ cups rice flour

2 teaspoons gluten-free baking powder

¾ cup superfine or granulated sugar

½ cup sunflower oil

1 cup buttermilk

2 extra-large eggs, beaten

¼ cup slivered almonds

Topping

1 cup cream cheese

2 tablespoons confectioners' sugar

2 tablespoons honey

1 Line a 12-cup muffin pan with paper muffin cups.

2 Put the apricots, orange juice and zest, and saffron into a small saucepan and simmer for 5 minutes, until tender. Transfer to a food processor or blender and blend to a puree. Set aside.

3 Mix the flour, baking powder, and sugar in a large bowl. Whisk together the oil, buttermilk, and eggs, then pour into the dry ingredients. Add the apricot puree and stir until just combined.

4 Spoon the batter into the muffin cups and sprinkle with the almonds. Place in a preheated oven, at 350°F, for about 20 minutes, until golden and springy to the touch. Transfer to a wire rack to cool.

5 Beat together the topping ingredients in a bowl, then spread over the cooled muffins.

velvet cupcakes with marshmallow topping

Makes 12

Preparation time 20 minutes, plus cooling

Cooking time 25–30 minutes

1⅓ cups brown rice flour

2 tablespoons cornstarch

3 tablespoons unsweetened cocoa powder, sifted

2 teaspoons gluten-free baking powder

½ teaspoon baking soda

6 tablespoons butter, softened

¾ cup plus 2 tablespoons superfine or granulated sugar

2 heaping teaspoons red food coloring paste

few drops of vanilla extract

2 eggs, beaten

1 cup buttermilk

1 teaspoon white wine vinegar

crumbled, freeze-dried raspberries, to serve

Marshmallow topping

1¼ cups granulated sugar

¼ cup light corn syrup

¼ cup water

4 extra-large egg whites

1 Line a 12-cup muffin pan with paper cupcake liners.

2 Stir together the flour, cornstarch, cocoa powder, baking powder, and baking soda in a bowl.

3 Beat together the butter and sugar in a large bowl until pale and fluffy, then stir in the food coloring and vanilla extract. Gradually add the eggs, then stir in the buttermilk and vinegar. Fold in the flour mixture.

4 Spoon the batter into the paper liners and place in a preheated oven, at 350°F, for 15–18 minutes, until risen and just firm to the touch. Transfer to a wire rack to cool.

5 Make the marshmallow topping. Put the sugar, syrup, and measured water into a large saucepan and heat gently, stirring, until the sugar has dissolved. Bring to a boil and simmer for about 5 minutes, until the mixture reaches 240°F on a candy thermometer. Remove the pan from the heat.

6 Whisk the egg whites in a large, clean bowl until they form stiff peaks, then gradually pour in the syrup mixture, whisking continuously for 10 minutes, until the topping is thick and glossy. Smooth topping over cooled cakes using the back of the spoon.

7 Sprinkle with the freeze-dried raspberries.

st. clement's madeleines

Makes 12

Preparation time 10 minutes,
  plus standing

Cooking time 8–10 minutes

butter, for greasing

½ cup rice flour, plus extra for dusting

2 eggs

⅓ cup superfine or granulated sugar

3 tablespoons cornstarch

½ teaspoon gluten-free baking powder

grated zest of 1 lemon

grated zest of 1 orange

1 stick butter, melted

confectioners' sugar, for dusting

These are best eaten warm, soon after baking, and they are delicious with a glass of milk.

1 Grease and flour a 12-section madeleine pan. Alternatively, grease and flour 20 cups of a mini muffin pan.

2 Whisk together the eggs and sugar in a large bowl until pale and creamy. Gently fold in all the remaining ingredients, then let stand for 20 minutes.

3 Spoon the batter into the prepared pan and place in a preheated oven, at 400°F, for 8–10 minutes, until springy to touch. Turn out onto a wire rack to cool slightly and lightly dust with confectioners' sugar. Serve warm.

Hints and tips

Try adding a tablespoon of unsweetened cocoa powder to the batter before resting to make chocolate orange madeleines.

orange & mixed berry friands

Makes 6

Preparation time 10 minutes

Cooking time 15–20 minutes

3 egg whites

1 cup confectioners' sugar, plus extra
  for dusting

2½ tablespoons rice flour

1 cup ground almonds (almond meal)

1 stick butter, melted

grated zest of 1 orange

12 blackberries

24 raspberries

1 Line a 6-cup muffin pan or friand pan with paper liners. Alternatively, grease the pans with butter.

2 Whisk the egg whites in a large, clean bowl until they are fluffy but not forming peaks. Stir in all the remaining ingredients except the fruit. Spoon the batter into the paper liners and top with the fruit.

3 Place in a preheated oven, at 350°F, for 15–20 minutes, until golden and slightly springy to the touch.

banana & peanut brownies

Makes 16

Preparation time 10 minutes

Cooking time 30–40 minutes

1¼ sticks butter, plus extra for greasing

7 oz gluten-free semisweet chocolate, broken into pieces

¾ cup plus 2 tablespoons superfine or granulated sugar

2 eggs

2 small ripe bananas, mashed

⅔ cup rice flour

1 teaspoon gluten-free baking powder

½ cup gluten-free white chocolate chips

3 tablespoons chunky peanut butter

Confectioners' sugar, for dusting

1 Grease and line an 8 inch square cake pan.

2 Melt the butter and semisweet chocolate in a large heatproof bowl set over a saucepan of gently simmering water, making sure the bottom of the bowl does not touch the water.

3 Beat together the sugar and eggs in a separate large bowl until pale and fluffy, then stir in the bananas, flour, baking powder, and chocolate chips. Fold in the melted chocolate mixture.

4 Pour the batter into the prepared pan, then dot over the peanut butter and swirl with a knife. Place in a preheated oven, at 350°F, for 25–35 minutes, until softly set. Let cool in the pan on a wire rack, then turn out and cut into squares. Serve dusted with confectioners' sugar.

cornmeal cake with curd & mascarpone topping

Serves 12

Preparation time 10 minutes, plus cooling

Cooking time 1–1¼ hours

2 sticks butter, softened, plus extra
   for greasing

1 cup superfine or granulated sugar

1 cup cornmeal

1 teaspoon gluten-free baking powder

2 cups ground almonds (almond meal)

3 eggs, beaten

grated zest 2 oranges

Topping

1 cup mascarpone cheese

¼ cup Lemon, Orange & Passion Fruit
   Curd (*see* page 30) or gluten-free
   lemon curd

1 Lightly grease and line a 9 inch round, deep cake pan.

2 Beat together the butter and sugar in a large bowl until pale and fluffy. Add all the remaining ingredients and combine until smooth.

3 Pour the batter into the prepared pan and place in a preheated oven, at 325°F, for 1–1¼ hours until golden and a toothpick inserted into the center comes out clean. Transfer to a wire rack to cool.

4 Beat together the mascarpone and the fruit curd in a bowl, then spread over the cooled cake.

lemon drizzle loaf

Serves 12

Preparation time 15 minutes

Cooking time 35–40 minutes

2 sticks butter, softened, plus extra
  for greasing

1¼ cups superfine or granulated sugar

1½ cups brown rice flour

2 teaspoons gluten-free baking powder

4 eggs, beaten

grated zest and juice of 1 lemon

lemon zest twist, to decorate (optional)

Lemon drizzle

grated zest and juice of 2 lemons

½ cup granulated sugar

1 Grease and line a 9 x 5 x 3 inch loaf pan.

2 Put all the cake ingredients except the lemon zest twist, if using, in a food processor and process until smooth, or beat together in a large bowl.

3 Spoon the batter into the prepared pan and place in a preheated oven, at 350°F, for 35–40 minutes, until golden and firm to the touch.

4 Prick holes all over the sponge with a toothpick. Mix together the drizzle ingredients in a bowl, then drizzle the liquid over the warm loaf. Let stand until completely cold. Decorate with a twist of lemon zest, if desired.

pear sheet cake

Serves 12

Preparation time 10 minutes

Cooking time 45 minutes

1¼ sticks butter, softened, plus extra
  for greasing

2 cups brown rice flour

2 teaspoons gluten-free baking powder

1 teaspoon ground cinnamon

1 cup packed light brown sugar

4 eggs

⅔ cup buttermilk

3 pears, peeled, cored, and sliced

Crumble topping

2 tablespoons brown rice flour

2 tablespoons cold butter, cubed

1 tablespoon Demerara or raw sugar

This will be just as popular with adults
as it is with kids and is the perfect
accompaniment to a cup of tea or coffee.

1 Grease and line an 8 x 12 inch baking pan.

2 Put all the cake ingredients except the pears into a food
processor and process until smooth, or beat together in a large
bowl. Pour the batter into the prepared pan, then arrange the
pears on top.

3 Make the crumble topping. Place the flour in a bowl, add
the butter, and rub in with the fingertips until the mixture
resembles fine bread crumbs. Stir in the sugar, then sprinkle it all
over the top of the cake batter.

4 Place in a preheated oven, at 350°F, for about 45 minutes,
until golden and just firm to the touch.

coconut & mango cake

Serves 12

Preparation time 15 minutes, plus cooling

Cooking time 45–50 minutes

1 stick butter, softened, plus extra
  for greasing

½ cup firmly packed light brown sugar

4 eggs, separated

1¾ cups buttermilk

1½ cups cornmeal

1¼ cups rice flour

2 teaspoons gluten-free baking powder

½ cup coconut milk powder

¾ cup flaked unsweetened dried coconut

1 mango, peeled, pitted and pureed

Filling

1 cup mascarpone cheese

1 mango, peeled, pitted, and
  finely chopped

2 tablespoons confectioners' sugar

1 Grease and line a 9 inch round, deep cake pan.

2 Beat together the butter and sugar in a large bowl until pale and fluffy, then beat in the egg yolks, buttermilk, cornmeal, flour, baking powder, coconut milk powder, and dried coconut.

3 Whisk the egg whites in a large clean bowl until they form soft peaks, then fold into the cake batter with the pureed mango.

4 Spoon the batter into the prepared pan and place in a preheated oven, at 400°F, for 45–50 minutes, until golden and firm to the touch. Transfer to a wire rack to cool.

5 Slice the cooled cake in half horizontally. Beat together all the filling ingredients in a bowl and spread half over 1 cake half, then sandwich together with the remaining cake half. Spread the remaining filling mixture over the top.

raspberry layer cake

Serves 12

Preparation time 10 minutes, plus cooling

Cooking time 20 minutes

1½ sticks butter, softened, plus extra
  for greasing

¾ cup plus 2 tablespoons superfine or
  granulated sugar

1 cup plus 2 tablespoons brown rice flour,
  plus extra for dusting

3 eggs

1 tablespoon gluten-free baking powder

few drops of vanilla extract

1 tablespoon milk

To decorate

¼ cup raspberry preserves or jam

confectioners' sugar

1 Grease and flour two 7 inch round cake pans.

2 Put all the cake ingredients into a food processor and process until smooth or beat together in a large bowl.

3 Spoon the batter into the prepared pans and place in a preheated oven, at 400°F, for about 20 minutes, until risen and golden. Transfer to a wire rack to cool.

4 Sandwich the cooled cakes together with the preserves and dust with confectioners' sugar.

cranberry cookies

Makes 30

Preparation time 10 minutes

Cooking time 12–15 minutes

½ cup polyunsaturated margarine

½ cup firmly packed light brown sugar

1 egg, beaten

¾ cup rice flour

¾ cup plus 1 tablespoon buckwheat flour

½ cup millet flakes

⅓ cup dried cranberries, chopped dried apricots, or raisins

For a treat, throw in some gluten-free chocolate chips with the fruit for fruity chocolate cookies.

1 Grease 3 baking sheets.

2 Beat together the margarine and sugar in a large bowl. Beat in the egg, then stir in all the remaining ingredients and combine to form a dough.

3 Place walnut-size balls of the dough on a baking sheet and press down with a fork.

4 Place in a preheated oven, at 350°F, for 12–15 minutes, until golden. Transfer to a wire rack to cool.

banana millet bars

Makes 12

Preparation time 5–10 minutes

Cooking time 20–25 minutes

1 stick butter, melted, plus extra for greasing

2 large ripe bananas

1 cup chopped dates

2 tablespoons light corn syrup

2 cups millet flakes

¾ cup hazelnuts, toasted and coarsely chopped

1 Lightly grease an 8 inch square baking pan.

2 Put the bananas into a bowl and mash well, then stir in all the remaining ingredients.

3 Press into the prepared pan and place in a preheated oven, at 350°F, for 20–25 minutes, until golden.

4 While still in the pan, mark into 12 bars, then let cool in the pan before turning out and breaking into bars.

Hints and tips

These will work well with any nuts that you have on hand. You can also include dried cranberries for an extra berry boost.

chocolate chip cookies

Makes 30

Preparation time 10 minutes

Cooking time 8–10 minutes

6 tablespoons butter, softened, plus extra
  for greasing

½ cup superfine or granulated sugar

⅓ cup firmly packed light brown sugar

1 egg, beaten

1 cup brown rice flour, plus extra
  for dusting

½ teaspoon baking soda

1 tablespoon unsweetened cocoa powder

½ cup gluten-free semisweet
  chocolate chips

1 Grease 3 baking sheets.

2 Put all the ingredients except the chocolate chips into a food processor and process until smooth, or beat together in a large bowl. Stir in the chocolate chips, then bring the mixture together to form a ball.

3 Turn out the dough on a surface lightly dusted with rice flour and divide into 30 equal balls. Place on the prepared sheets, well spaced apart, pressing down gently with the back of a fork.

4 Place in a preheated oven, at 350°F, for 8–10 minutes. Let harden on the baking sheets for a few minutes, then transfer to a wire rack to cool.

buttery shortbread

Makes 12

Preparation time 10 minutes

Cooking time 10–12 minutes

1 stick butter, softened, plus extra
 for greasing

¼ cup superfine or granulated sugar

⅔ cup rice flour

¾ cup cornstarch

Demerara or raw sugar, for sprinkling

1 Grease an 11 x 7 inch baking pan.

2 Beat together the butter and sugar in a bowl until pale and fluffy, then stir in the flour and cornstarch and combine to form a dough.

3 Press the dough into the prepared pan and prick all over with a fork. Sprinkle with the Demerara sugar.

4 Place in a preheated oven, at 400°F, for 10–12 minutes, until golden.

5 While still in the pan, mark into 12 bars, then let cool in the pan before turning out and breaking into bars.

Hints and tips

This basic shortbread recipe can be varied. Try chocolate shortbread—replace the rice and cornstarch with buckwheat flour and add 2 tablespoons unsweetened cocoa powder. Or you could make nutty spiced shortbread— add 1 teaspoon allspice and the grated zest of 1 orange to the basic mixture, then press 1½ cups chopped mixed nuts into the dough after it has been pressed into the pan.

fruity mango millet bars

Makes 12

Preparation time 10 minutes

Cooking time 35 minutes

1¼ sticks butter, plus extra for greasing

½ cup packed light brown sugar

2 tablespoons light corn syrup

2 cups millet flakes

2 tablespoons mixed pumpkin and
  sunflower seeds

⅔ cup coarsely chopped dried mango

1 Grease an 11 x 7 inch baking pan.

2 Put the sugar, butter, and syrup into a heavy saucepan and heat until melted, then stir in the remaining ingredients.

3 Spoon the batter into the prepared pan and press down lightly. Place in a preheated oven, at 300°F, for 30 minutes.

4 While still in the pan, mark into 12 bars, then place on a wire rack to cool completely before turning out and breaking into bars.

basic white loaf

Makes 1 loaf

Preparation time 10 minutes, plus proving

Cooking time 35–40 minutes

2¼ teaspoons or 1 (¼ oz) envelope active dry yeast

1 tablespoon granulated sugar

1¼ cups warm water

½ teaspoon salt

1 teaspoon gluten-free baking powder

¼ cup instant dry milk

1⅓ cups potato starch

2 cups rice flour

⅓ cup cornstarch

1 tablespoon xanthan gum

2 eggs, beaten

¼ cup vegetable oil

1 Line a 9 x 5 x 3 inch loaf pan.

2 Put the yeast, sugar, and ½ cup of the warm water in a small bowl and set aside for about 10 minutes, until frothy.

3 Stir together the salt, baking powder, dry milk, potato starch, flour, cornstarch, and xanthan gum in a large bowl. Mix together the eggs, oil, and remaining water in a separate bowl, then stir into the yeast mixture and add to the dry ingredients. Combine to form a dough, adding a little extra water or flour, if necessary.

4 Pour into the prepared pan and level the top. Spritz with a little water, then let rest in a warm place to rise for about 1½ hours, until it comes to the top of the pan.

5 Place in a preheated oven, at 400°F, for 15 minutes, then reduce the temperature to 350°F and bake for an additional 20–25 minutes, until the loaf is golden and firm to touch. Let cool in the pan for 10 minutes, then turn out onto a wire rack to cool.

cheese, apple & walnut bread

Makes 1 loaf

Preparation time 15 minutes

Cooking time 40–45 minutes

1½ cups rice flour, plus extra for dusting

1⅔ cups buckwheat flour

3 tablespoons cold butter, cubed

1 large crisp sweet apple, peeled, cored, and finely chopped

1½ cups sharp cheddar cheese

¾ cup coarsely chopped walnuts

2 tablespoons chopped chives

½–⅔ cup skim milk

beaten egg, to glaze

salt and black pepper

1 Lightly dust a baking sheet with rice flour.

2 Sift the flours into a large bowl, tipping any bran remaining in the sifter into the bowl. Add the butter and rub in with the fingertips until the mixture resembles fine bread crumbs. Season well. Using a fork, stir in the apple, cheese, walnuts, and chives, then add enough of the milk to form a soft dough.

3 Turn out the dough onto a surface lightly dusted with rice flour and shape into a disk about 8 inches in diameter. Brush with the beaten egg, then cut a lattice pattern into the top using a sharp knife.

4 Transfer to the prepared baking sheet and place in a preheated oven, at 375°F, for 35–40 minutes, until golden. Turn the loaf over and bake for an additional 5 minutes. Serve warm.

cheesy bread

Makes 1 loaf

**Preparation time 10 minutes,
  plus proving**

Cooking time 45 minutes

1½ cups cornmeal

⅔ cup rice flour

¾ cup instant dry milk

2¼ teaspoons or 1 (¼ oz) envelope
  active dry yeast

1 teaspoon granulated sugar

2 teaspoons xanthan gum

¼ cup grated Parmesan cheese

1 cup shredded sharp cheddar cheese

3 eggs, beaten

2 cups lukewarm water

1 Line a 9 x 5 x 3 inch loaf pan.

2 Stir together the cornmeal, flour, milk powder, yeast, sugar, xanthan gum, and cheeses in a large bowl. Mix together the eggs and water in a small bowl, then pour into the dry ingredients and stir together to form a sticky dough.

3 Pour the dough into the prepared pan, cover with a clean, damp dish towel, and let rise in a warm place for 30–45 minutes, until the dough is near the top of the pan.

4 Place in a preheated oven, at 350°F, for about 45 minutes or until golden and it sounds hollow when tapped on the bottom. Transfer to a wire rack to cool.

cheesy herb muffins

Makes 8

Preparation time 10 minutes

Cooking time 20 minutes

1½ cups shredded Gruyère cheese

3 scallions, finely sliced

1 teaspoon thyme leaves

1 tablespoon chopped parsley

¾ cup rice flour

½ teaspoon gluten-free baking powder

3 cups fresh gluten-free bread crumbs

1 teaspoon gluten-free English mustard

3 eggs, beaten

4 tablespoons butter, melted

¼ cup milk

1 Line 8 cups of a muffin pan with paper muffin cups.

2 Mix together all the ingredients in a large bowl until just combined.

3 Spoon the batter into the muffin cups and place in a preheated oven, at 375°F, for 20 minutes or until golden and just firm to the touch. Serve warm.

corn & bacon muffins

Makes 12

Preparation time 10 minutes

Cooking time 20–25 minutes

3 tablespoons vegetable oil, plus extra
  for greasing

6 bacon slices, finely chopped

1 small red onion, finely chopped

1⅓ cups frozen corn kernels

1¼ cups fine cornmeal

¾ cup rice flour

2 teaspoons gluten-free baking powder

½ cup shredded cheddar cheese

1 cup milk

2 eggs, beaten

1 Grease a 12-cup muffin pan with oil.

2 Heat a skillet, add the bacon and onion, and dry-fry for 3–4 minutes, until the bacon is turning crisp.

3 Meanwhile, cook the corn kernels in a saucepan of boiling water for 2 minutes to soften. Drain well.

4 Mix together the cornmeal, flour, and baking powder in a bowl, then stir in the corn, cheese, bacon, and onion. Whisk together the milk, eggs, and oil in a separate small bowl, then pour into the dry ingredients and stir until just combined.

5 Pour the batter into the cups in the prepared pan and place in a preheated oven, at 425°F, for 15–20 minutes, until golden and just firm to the touch. Transfer to a wire rack to cool.

soda bread

Makes 1 loaf

Preparation time 10 minutes

Cooking time 30–35 minutes

1½ cups white rice flour, plus extra for dusting

¾ cup tapioca (cassava) flour

1 tablespoon superfine or granulated sugar

2 tablespoons instant dry milk

1 teaspoon baking soda

1 teaspoon gluten-free baking powder

1 teaspoon salt

1 egg, beaten

1¼ cups buttermilk

This loaf is so easy to make and wonderful served hot with butter or toasted, perfect for Sunday brunch.

1 Sift all the dry ingredients into a large bowl. Whisk together the egg and buttermilk in a separate small bowl, then stir into the dry ingredients and use your fingertips to form a dough.

2 Turn out the dough onto a surface lightly dusted with rice flour and shape into a disk. Place on a dusted baking sheet and make a large cross across the top of the dough, using a sharp knife. Sprinkle with a little extra flour.

3 Place in an oven preheated to its highest setting for 5 minutes, then reduce the temperature to 350°F and bake for an additional 25–30 minutes or until it sounds hollow when tapped on the bottom.

simple banana cheesecake

Serves 4

Preparation time 10 minutes, plus chilling

32 amaretti cookies (about 5 oz), or other gluten-free cookies, crushed

4 tablespoons butter, melted

3 bananas, sliced

1¼ cups cream cheese

2 tablespoons confectioners' sugar

⅓ cup dulce de leche or caramel sauce

This combination of banana and caramel in a cheesecake is delicious and indulgent, a real winner for all the family.

1 Mix together the crushed cookies and melted butter in a bowl, then press into an 8 inch loose-bottom or springform pan. Chill for 20 minutes.

2 Arrange the sliced bananas over the cookie crust. Beat together all the remaining ingredients in a bowl, then spread over the bananas.

3 Chill for at least 30 minutes before serving.

spiced pear & apple crisp

Serves 4

Preparation time 10 minutes

Cooking time 30–35 minutes

4 Bosc pears (about 1½ lb), peeled, cored, and sliced

3 cooking apples, such as Granny Smith, peeled, cored, and sliced

2 tablespoons packed light brown sugar

1 teaspoon ground cinnamon

¼ cup apple juice

crème fraîche or whipped cream, to serve

Topping

1¼ cups rice flour

1 stick cold butter, cubed

½ cup packed brown sugar

¼ cup slivered almonds

¼ cup blanched hazelnuts, coarsely chopped

1 Put the pears and apples into a large saucepan with the sugar, cinnamon, and apple juice. Cover and cook gently for about 10 minutes, stirring occasionally, until the fruit is just tender. Transfer to an ovenproof dish.

2 Make the topping. Put the flour and butter into a food processor and process until the mixture resembles fine bread crumbs. Alternatively, put the flour into a large bowl, add the butter, and rub in with the fingertips until the mixture resembles fine bread crumbs. Stir in the sugar and nuts, then sprinkle it over the fruit and press down gently.

3 Place in a preheated oven, at 400°F, for 20–25 minutes, until golden and bubbling. Serve with crème fraîche or whipped cream.

rhubarb & custard ice cream

Serves 6

Preparation time 15 minutes, plus cooling and freezing

Cooking time 20 minutes

9 rhubarb stalks (about 1 lb), cut into 2½ inch chunks

1½ cups superfine or granulated sugar

2 tablespoons water

5 egg yolks

1¼ cups heavy cream

1¼ cups milk

few drops of vanilla extract

1 Put the rhubarb, ⅓ cup of the sugar and the measured water into a small saucepan. Cover and cook over low heat for about 10 minutes, until the rhubarb is tender. Let cool slightly, then put into a food processor or blender and blend to a puree. Set aside.

2 Whisk the remaining sugar and egg yolks in a heatproof bowl until thick and pale. Heat the cream, milk, and vanilla extract in a saucepan until hot, then whisk into the sugar mixture. Return the mixture to the pan and heat gently, stirring continuously, until the custard is thickened—do not let it boil.

3 Remove the pan from the heat, cover with plastic wrap, and let the custard cool.

4 When the custard is completely cold, stir in the rhubarb puree and transfer to a freezerproof container. Freeze for 2 hours, then whisk the mixture to remove any ice crystals and return to the freezer for an additional 2 hours. Whisk again, then freeze until solid.

rhubarb sheet cake

Serves 8

Preparation time 10 minutes

Cooking time 20 minutes

½ cup polyunsaturated margarine,
  plus extra for greasing

2 tablespoons light corn syrup

1 tablespoon packed light brown sugar

¾ cup millet flakes

½ cup buckwheat flour

pinch of ground ginger

¼ cup chopped pecans

⅓ cup rhubarb compote or stewed
  rhubarb (*see* Step 1 opposite)

1 Put the margarine, syrup, and sugar into a saucepan and heat gently until the sugar has dissolved. Stir in the millet flakes, flour, ginger, and pecans and combine well.

2 Press two-thirds of the batter into a 6 inch square, greased baking pan and gently press down. Spoon the rhubarb over the batter, then sprinkle with the remaining millet mixture and press down lightly.

3 Place in a preheated oven, at 350°F, for 15–20 minutes, until the top is golden.

upside-down banana tart

Serves 6

Preparation time 15 minutes, plus chilling

Cooking time 30–35 minutes

4 tablespoons butter

½ cup superfine or granulated sugar

5 firm bananas, halved lengthwise

cream or ice cream, to serve

Pastry dough

¾ cup rice flour, plus extra for dusting

2 tablespoons cornmeal

6 tablespoons cold butter, cubed

1 tablespoon superfine or granulated
  sugar

1 egg yolk

1 Make the pastry dough. Put the flour, cornmeal, butter, and sugar into a food processor and process until the mixture resembles fine bread crumbs. Alternatively, mix together the rice flour and cornmeal in a large bowl. Add the butter and rub in with the fingertips until the mixture resembles fine bread crumbs, then stir in the sugar. Add the egg yolk and enough water to form a dough.

2 Meanwhile, melt the butter in a heavy 9 inch ovenproof skillet. Add the sugar and cook over medium heat until it has turned a golden caramel color. Let cool slightly, then arrange the bananas in the pan, cut side up (you may have to cut a few pieces a little smaller to fit the pan).

3 Turn out the dough on a surface lightly dusted with rice flour and roll out to a disk a little bigger than the skillet. Lay the dough over the bananas and tuck in the sides.

4 Place in a preheated oven, at 425°F, for 25–30 minutes or until golden and starting to bubble around the sides.

5 Carefully invert onto a serving plate and serve with cream or ice cream.

crunchy plum slump

Serves 4–6

Preparation time 15 minutes

Cooking time 20–25 minutes

10 plums (about 1½ lb), halved, pitted, and quartered

½ teaspoon ground ginger

¼ cup superfine or granulated sugar

grated zest and juice of 1 orange

¼ cup mascarpone cheese

1 cup brown rice flour

4 tablespoons butter or ¼ cup margarine, cubed

2 tablespoons packed soft brown sugar

grated zest of ½ lemon

⅓ cup milk

1 Put the plums, ginger, superfine sugar, and the orange zest and juice into a medium saucepan and bring to a boil, then simmer gently for 5–6 minutes, until the plums are just tender. Transfer to an ovenproof dish and spoon over blobs of mascarpone.

2 Put the flour into a bowl, add the butter or margarine, and rub in with fingertips until the mixture resembles bread crumbs. Stir in the brown sugar, lemon zest, and milk until combined. Drop spoonfuls of the batter over the plums and mascarpone.

3 Place in a preheated oven, at 400°F, for 15–20 minutes, until golden and bubbling.

cheesy bites

Makes about 48

Preparation time 15 minutes, plus chilling

Cooking time 12–15 minutes

¾ cup rice flour, plus extra for dusting

⅓ cup cornstarch

1 stick cold butter, cubed

¾ cup shredded sharp cheddar cheese

2 tablespoons grated Parmesan cheese

1 egg yolk

1 Put the flour, cornstarch, and butter into a food processor and process until the mixture resembles fine bread crumbs. Alternatively, place the flour and cornstarch into a large bowl, add the butter, and rub in with the fingertips until the mixture resembles fine bread crumbs. Stir in the cheddar and half of the Parmesan. Add the egg yolk and enough water to form a dough.

2 Turn out the dough onto a surface lightly dusted with rice flour and roll out to a rectangle about ¼ inch thick. Cut out small shapes, such as stars or disks (because they will be crumbly, it is best to keep the shapes small so that the bites are more stable). Transfer to a greased baking sheet and sprinkle with the remaining Parmesan.

3 Place in a preheated oven, at 350°F, for 12–15 minutes, until golden. Transfer to a wire rack to cool.

parmesan & mixed seed pops

Makes 12

Preparation time 10 minutes

Cooking time 3–5 minutes

2 cups grated Parmesan cheese

2 tablespoons sesame seeds

1 tablespoon poppy seeds

1 tablespoon sunflower or pumpkin seeds

pinch of cayenne pepper (optional)

1 Line 2 baking sheets with nonstick parchment paper.

2 Mix together all the ingredients in a bowl, then spoon onto the prepared baking sheets to form 12 mounds, spaced well apart. Press an ice cream stick into each mounds so that part of the sticks are covered with a little of the mixture.

3 Place in a preheated oven, at 400°F, for 3–5 minutes, until golden and lacy. Let cool on the baking sheets, then serve.

pizza scrolls

Makes 8

Preparation time 25 minutes,
  plus proving

Cooking time 12–15 minutes

1½ tablespoons or 2 (¼ oz) envelopes
  active dry yeast

1 teaspoon superfine or granulated sugar

1 cup milk, warmed

1 cup plus 2 tablespoons rice flour,
  plus extra for dusting

1 cup plus 2 tablespoons potato flour

1 teaspoon gluten-free baking powder

1 teaspoon xanthan gum

pinch of salt

1 tablespoon sunflower oil, plus extra
  for oiling

1 egg, beaten

Filling

¼ cup tomato puree or tomato sauce

2 cups shredded mixed mozzarella and
  cheddar cheese

3 oz wafer-thin ham, shredded

handful of basil, chopped

1 Put the yeast, sugar, and milk into a bowl and set aside for about 10 minutes, until frothy.

2 Stir together the flours, baking powder, xanthan gum, and salt in a large bowl. Mix together the oil and egg in a separate bowl, stir into the yeast mixture, and add this to the dry ingredients. Combine to form a soft dough.

3 Turn out the dough onto a surface lightly dusted with rice flour and knead for 5 minutes, adding a little rice flour if the mixture becomes sticky. Put into a lightly oiled bowl, cover with a clean, damp dish towel, and let rise in a warm place for 40 minutes or until well risen.

4 Lightly oil a heavy baking sheet or pan. Roll the dough out on the floured surface to a rectangle about 12 x 10 inches, spread with the tomato puree or sauce, then sprinkle with the remaining filling ingredients. Roll the pizza up from one long edge, then slice into 8 pieces.

5 Place the rolled-up pizza scrolls side by side on the prepared baking sheet or pan. They should be pushed up against each other so that the sides are touching. Place in a preheated oven, at 425°F, for 12–15 minutes, until golden. Serve warm.

scrumptious sausage rolls

Makes 20

Preparation time 20 minutes, plus chilling

Cooking time 18–20 minutes

6 gluten-free sausage links, skins removed

handful of fresh herbs, such as chives and parsley, chopped (optional)

milk, for brushing

Pastry dough

1¼ cups brown rice flour, plus extra for dusting

⅓ cup cornmeal

½ teaspoon xanthan gum

1 stick cold butter, cubed

1 egg yolk

1 Make the pastry dough. Put the flour, cornmeal, xanthan gum, and butter into a food processor and process until the mixture resembles bread crumbs. Alternatively, mix together the dry ingredients in a large bowl. Add the butter and rub in with the fingertips until the mixture resembles bread crumbs. Add the egg yolk and enough water to form a dough. Knead the dough for a few minutes, then wrap in plastic wrap and chill for 30 minutes.

2 Meanwhile, put the sausagemeat and herbs into a bowl and mix well.

3 Turn out the pastry onto a surface lightly dusted with rice flour and roll out to a rectangle about 9½ x 18¾ inches. Cut in half to form 2 smaller rectangles.

4 Divide the meat into 2 pieces and shape into long rolls the same length as the dough. Lay 1 sausage roll on each piece of dough, then wet the dough edges with milk and fold over and press down to encase the meat and seal the edges. Cut each strip into about 10 smaller sausage rolls, then snip the top of each with scissors to make a V shape. Brush the sausage rolls with milk.

5 Transfer the sausage rolls to a greased baking sheet and place in a preheated oven, at 400°F, for 18–20 minutes, until golden and cooked through.

kid-friendly mince pies

Makes 12

Preparation time 15 minutes, plus chilling

Cooking time 15–20 minutes

⅔ cup golden raisins

⅓ cup chopped dried mango

¾ cups almonds, toasted and chopped

2 tablespoons honey

2 tablespoons cream cheese

milk, for brushing

Pastry dough

1 cup rice flour, plus extra for dusting

3 tablespoons cornmeal

6 tablespoons cold butter, cubed

2 tablespoons superfine or granulated
   sugar

1 egg yolk

grated zest of 1 orange

1 Make the pastry dough. Put the flour, cornmeal, butter, and sugar into a food processor and process until the mixture resembles fine bread crumbs. Alternatively, mix together the rice flour and cornmeal in a bowl. Add the butter and rub in with the fingertips until the mixture resembles fine bread crumbs, then stir in the sugar. Add the egg, orange zest, and enough cold water to form a dough. Wrap in plastic wrap and chill for 30 minutes.

2 Mix together the golden raisins, mango, almonds, honey, and cream cheese in a bowl.

3 Roll out the dough between 2 sheets of wax paper or plastic wrap. Cut out 12 disks, using a 3 inch pastry cutter and 12 disks using a 2½ inch pastry cutter, rerolling the scraps, if necessary.

4 Use the large disks to line a 12-cup muffine pan. Divide the cream cheese mixture evenly among the shells, cover with the smaller dough lids and press gently to seal the edges. Brush the tops with a little milk and cut a slit in each.

5 Place in a preheated oven, at 350°F, for 15–20 minutes, until golden.

lemon & raspberry cupcakes

Makes 12

Preparation time 10 minutes

Cooking time 12–15 minutes

1¼ sticks butter, softened

¾ cup superfine or granulated sugar

½ cup rice flour

⅔ cup cornstarch

1 tablespoon gluten-free baking powder

grated zest and juice of 1 lemon

3 eggs, beaten

1 cup raspberries

1 tablespoon gluten-free lemon curd

1 Line a 12-cup muffin pan with paper cupcake liners.

2 Beat together all the ingredients except the raspberries and lemon curd in a large bowl. Fold in the raspberries.

3 Spoon half the batter into the cupcake liners, dot with a little of the lemon curd, then divide the remaining batter among the cupcake liners.

4 Place in a preheated oven, at 400°F, for 12–15 minutes, until golden and firm to the touch. Transfer to a wire rack to cool.

orange animal cookies

Makes 20

Preparation time 15 minutes, plus cooling

Cooking time 10 minutes

1¼ cups brown rice flour, plus extra
  for dusting

½ teaspoon xanthan gum

1 teaspoon gluten-free baking powder

4 tablespoons butter, cubed

¼ cup firmly packed light brown sugar

grated zest of 1 orange

1 egg, beaten

2 tablespoons light corn syrup

To decorate

1¼ cups confectioners' sugar

1 tablespoon boiling water

liquid food coloring (optional)

gluten-free candies

1 Line 2 baking sheets with nonstick parchment paper.

2 Put the flour, xanthan gum, baking powder, and butter into a food processor and process until the mixture resembles fine bread crumbs. Alternatively, mix together the flour, xanthan gum, and baking powder in a large bowl. Add the butter and rub in with the fingertips until the mixture resembles fine bread crumbs. Stir in the sugar and orange zest. Add the egg and corn syrup and combine to form a firm dough.

3 Turn out the dough onto a surface lightly dusted with rice flour and roll out to ¼ inch thick. Using animal cutters, cut out 20 cookies, rerolling the scraps as necessary.

4 Transfer the cookies to the prepared baking sheets and place in a preheated oven, at 325°F, for about 10 minutes, until golden. Let harden on the baking sheets for a few minutes, then transfer to a wire rack to cool.

5 Mix the confectioners' sugar with the boiling water and add the food coloring, if using, then smooth over the cooled cookies or pipe icing details. Decorate with candies and let set.

scary halloween cookies

Makes 12–14

Preparation time 15 minutes, plus cooling

Cooking time 12–15 minutes

1 stick butter, softened

½ cup firmly packed light brown sugar

1 egg yolk

1 teaspoon ground ginger

1¼ cups rice flour, plus extra for dusting

⅔ cup cornstarch

To decorate

10 oz ready-to-use rolled fondant

confectioners' sugar, for dusting

icing pens

Use any shaped cookie cutter you want, such as bats or gingerbread men (you can cut off the heads, legs, or arms to make them scary). Choose icing colors to correspond with the cookie shapes—for example, black if you are making bats.

1 Beat together the butter and sugar in a large bowl until pale and fluffy, then gradually beat in the egg yolk. Sift the ginger, flour, and cornstarch into a separate bowl, then fold into the creamed mixture and form into a ball.

2 Turn out the dough onto a surface lightly dusted with rice flour and roll out to ¼ inch thick. Cut out shapes using cookie cutters, rerolling the scraps, if necessary, and transfer to 2 baking sheets.

3 Place in a preheated oven, at 375°F, for 12–15 minutes, until beginning to turn golden. Transfer to a wire rack to cool.

4 To decorate the cooled cookies, roll out the fondant on a surface dusted with confectioners' sugar and cut out shapes using the cookie cutters. Place on top of the cookies and add details, using the icing pens.

chocolate cake with buttercream

Serves 8

Preparation time 10 minutes, plus cooling

Cooking time 12–15 minutes

2 sticks butter, softened, plus extra for greasing

1 cup plus 2 tablespoons superfine or granulated sugar

1¼ cups rice flour

¼ cup unsweetened cocoa powder

4 eggs

2 teaspoons gluten-free baking powder

2 tablespoons milk

Frosting

1¼ sticks butter, softened

2 cups confectioners' sugar

2 tablespoons unsweetened cocoa powder

For a special occasion, decorate the cake with gluten-free candies or shavings of chocolate. If you prefer a vanilla cake, increase the amount of rice flour by 3 tablespoons and replace the cocoa powder with a few drops of vanilla extract.

1 Lightly grease and line two 8 inch cake pans.

2 Place all the cake ingredients into a food processor and process until smooth, or beat together in a large bowl.

3 Divide the batter between the prepared pans and place in a preheated oven, at 350°F, for 12–15 minutes, until just firm to the touch and beginning to shrink away from the sides of the pans. Transfer to a wire rack to cool.

4 Beat together all the frosting ingredients in a bowl, then spread half over 1 cake and sandwich together with the remaining cake. Spread the remaining frosting over the top.

zebra cakes

Makes 12

Preparation time 15 minutes, plus cooling

Cooking time 15–18 minutes

2 sticks butter or 1 cup margarine,
softened

1¼ cups superfine or granulated sugar

1½ cups brown rice flour

4 eggs

2 tablespoons unsweetened cocoa
powder

Frosting

1¼ sticks butter

2⅓ cups confectioners' sugar

1 tablespoon unsweetened cocoa powder

a little milk

1 Line a 12-cup muffin pan with paper muffin cups.

2 Place the butter or margarine, superfine sugar, flour, and eggs in a food processor and process until pale and smooth, or beat together in a large bowl. Spoon out half the batter into a separate bowl and beat in the cocoa powder.

3 Place the cake batter into 2 separate pastry bags fitted with plain tips. Pipe alternate layers of cake batter into each cup.

4 Place in a preheated oven, at 400°F, for 15–18 minutes, until risen and just firm to the touch. Transfer to a wire rack to cool.

5 Beat together all the frosting ingredients in a bowl, adding just enough milk to form a soft, smooth consistency. Pipe or spread the frosting onto the cooled zebra cakes.

Hints and tips
You can add orange flavoring to the frosting instead of cocoa powder.

chocolate caramel shortbread

Makes 15

Preparation time 20 minutes, plus cooling and chilling

Cooking time 15 minutes

1 stick butter, softened, plus extra
  for greasing

¼ cup superfine or granulated sugar

⅔ cup brown rice flour

¾ cup cornstarch

Caramel

1 stick butter

¼ cup firmly packed light brown sugar

1 (14 oz) can condensed milk

Topping

4 oz gluten-free white chocolate

4 oz gluten-free semisweet chocolate

1 Grease an 11 x 7 inch baking pan.

2 Beat together the butter and sugar in a large bowl until pale and fluffy, then stir in the rice flour and cornstarch until well combined.

3 Press the shortbread into the prepared pan and place in a preheated oven, at 400°F, for 10–12 minutes, until golden.

4 Meanwhile, place all the caramel ingredients into a heavy saucepan and heat over low heat until the sugar has dissolved, then cook for 5 minutes, stirring continuously. Remove the pan from the heat and let cool slightly.

5 Remove the shortbread from the oven, pour the caramel over it, and let cool until set.

6 Melt the white and semisweet chocolate in separate heatproof bowls set over saucepans of gently simmering water, making sure the bottoms of the bowls do not touch the water. When the caramel is firm, spoon alternate spoonfuls of the white and semisweet chocolate over the caramel, tap the pan on the work surface so that the different chocolates merge, then use a knife to make swirls in the chocolate.

7 Chill until set, then cut the shortbread into 15 squares.

lemon meringue frozen yogurt

Serves 6

Preparation time 5 minutes, plus freezing

2 cups Greek yogurt

2 tablespoons confectioners' sugar

¼ cup gluten-free lemon curd

2 meringue nests, crushed

grated zest of 1 lemon

1 Put all the ingredients in a bowl and gently mix together until combined.

2 Transfer the mixture to a freezerproof container and freeze until solid.

super simple vanilla ice cream

Serves 6

Preparation time 5 minutes, plus freezing

1⅓ cups prepared custard or vanilla pudding filling

1¼ cups heavy cream

This is a simple recipe that can be easily adapted by adding fruit purees or flavorings of your choice.

1 Put the custard and cream into a bowl and stir together, then transfer the mixture to a freezerproof container.

2 Freeze for 2 hours, then whisk the mixture to remove any ice crystals and return to the freezer for an additional 2 hours. Whisk again, then freeze until solid.

fruity ice pops

Makes 4

Preparation time 5 minutes, plus freezing

2 cups raspberries, defrosted if frozen

2 ripe bananas, chopped

1 cup Greek yogurt

3 tablespoons honey

1 Put all the ingredients into a food processor or blender and process until smooth, then spoon the mixture into 4 ice pop molds.

2 Freeze until solid.

Hints and tips

These work with any fruit, so experiment with different combinations to find your kids' favorite flavor. It's a great way to add fruit to their diet.

salted caramel popcorn

Serves 4

Preparation time 5 minutes

Cooking time 10 minutes

1 teaspoon sunflower oil

¼ cup popping corn

1 cup granulated sugar

2 tablespoons of butter

sea salt flakes

1 Heat the oil in a large lidded saucepan. Add the popping corn, cover, and heat, shaking the pan frequently until the corn has all popped. Transfer to a large sheet of nonstick parchment paper.

2 Put the sugar into a saucepan and heat over low heat until the sugar has dissolved. Simmer until golden, then stir in the butter. Drizzle the caramel over the popcorn and sprinkle with a little salt.

grilled fruit kebabs

Makes 8

Preparation time 10 minutes, plus soaking

Cooking time 5–6 minutes

3 tablespoons butter, melted

2 tablespoons maple syrup

pinch of ground ginger

2 large firm bananas, cut into chunks

1 papaya, peeled, seeded, and cut into chunks

1 small pineapple, peeled, cored, and cut into chunks

cream or yogurt, to serve

1 Presoak 8 wooden skewers in water for 30 minutes.

2 Mix together the butter, syrup, and ginger in a small bowl. Thread the fruit alternately onto the skewers, then brush with the syrup mixture.

3 Cook under a preheated hot broiler or on a barbecue grill for 5–6 minutes, turning and brushing with syrup occasionally, until golden and beginning to char. Serve with cream or yogurt.

berry smoothie gelatins

Serves 4

Preparation time 10 minutes,
plus soaking and chilling

Cooking time 3 minutes

6 sheets of gelatin

2 cups berry smoothie juice

⅔ cup fruit yogurt

2 cups berries, such as blueberries,
raspberries, or hulled strawberries

Try pairing the smoothies with different fruits. You can use almost any flavor smoothie to make the gelatines, but acidic foods, such as pineapple, will not produce a good gelatin set.

1 Soak the gelatin in a bowl of cold water according to package directions until soft and floppy, then transfer the mixture to a small saucepan and heat gently until melted. Gradually stir in the smoothie and yogurt.

2 Divide the berries among 4 tall glasses, then pour over the smoothie mixture. Chill until set.

index

acknowledgments

Publisher's credits

Octopus Publishing Group would like to thank all the children featured in this book:
Evie Coughlan, Charlie Killick, Isaac Odeniyi, Sofia Rajah, Ameliah Rajah, Freddie Shaw,
Grace Shaw, and Oscar Byrnes Taylor.

Picture credits

Special photography by William Shaw.
Other photography:
Fotolia Tombaky 4 background (used throughout).
Octopus Publishing Group Vanessa Davies 91, 95; Emma Neish 99, 103, 107, 109, 131;
Lis Parsons 71; Craig Robertson 18, 69, 82, 115; William Shaw 14, 15, 27, 39, 44, 60, 68, 75,
83, 84, 114, 119.

Commissioning Editor: **Sarah Ford**
Editor: **Pauline Bache**
Art Director: **Tracy Killick at Tracy Killick Art Direction and Design**
Photographer: **William Shaw**
Home economist: **Louise Blair**
Prop Stylist: **Tony Hutchinson at Refresh**
Picture Library Manager: **Jennifer Veall**
Assistant Production Manager: **John Casey**